FOUNDATIONS FOR TRUE AND COMPLETE
DELIVERANCE

UNDERSTANDING HOW DELIVERANCE

WORKS SERIES

PATRICK I. ODIGIE

FOUNDATIONS FOR TRUE AND COMPLETE

First Printing – May 2017

Published by: Prophetic Power House Inc. New York

Editing and Layout Design
Cornerstone Publishing
info@thecornerstonepublishers.com
www.thecornerstonepublishers.com

Cover design by Bodunrin Akinyanju

For more copies of this book and all our messages and training materials please contact:
Patrick I. Odigie
Post Office Box 830, Uniondale NY 11553
516 499-2350
Email: propheticpowerhouse@yahoo.com
Website: www.patrickodigie.com

FOREWORD

I consider it a great honor to be asked to write a foreword to this amazing book. I have known Rev. Patrick Odigie for over 30 years, both as a close friend, and co-minister in the service of God's Kingdom. Rev. Odigie is a widely respected minister of the Gospel with unusual teaching and prophetic insights. God has also blessed him with a special anointing to minister healing and deliverance to the sick and oppressed.

This book, Foundations for True and Effective Deliverance, has been written in response to the silent and vocal cries of many of God's people (including mine) for a balanced, insightful and inspirational reference on the subject of deliverance. The book lays a clear overview of the subject; it is also a fantastic resource and user guide covering varied and rarely addressed dimensions of the subject.

When Rev. Odigie made a decision to write this book, I was in no doubt about the scope, depth and clarity it will add to one of the most debated, yet all-important Christian subjects. In many respects the author has made a new and scarce contribution to the topic, and I hope it will serve as an eye opener to the subject of deliverance- an area in which the devil has exploited the ignorance and laid-back attitude of God's people for too long.

For Christians who do not believe in deliverance ministry, I invite them to read this book with an open heart and have a re-think about their position. For believers who have unanswered questions about deliverance, this book will help clear the air and dispel many of the doubts in their hearts. And, for the rest of us who have absolute confidence that deliverance is God's will for His people, Foundations for True and Effective Deliverance, will provide additional learning and a reliable reference as we flip through its pages.

I have found this book a clear, rare and distinctive contribution to one of the most important aspects of Christianity. I strongly recommend it for everyone whatever your position, experience and calling in God's Kingdom. God bless as you read.

Jerome Obode
Senior Pastor, Global Impact Tabernacle,
London, United Kingdom.

DEDICATION

To the one Eternal God, the Creator of all things, both visible and invisible.

To the Lord Jesus who loves me completely; going all the way, He drank the full cup of the wrath of the Almighty God in my stead.

And to the Blessed Eternal Spirit of grace, my Counselor, Teacher and ever patient Coach, be all the glory always, now and forever! I love you till eternity my God.

ACKNOWLEDGMENTS

In Africa, we say, "it takes a village to raise a child". To stay on the true path of life and attempting to share some beneficial truths through these series is made possible by three generations of generous human beings whose love, sacrifice, and faith in me has greatly enriched my life's' journey and purpose. Standing strong with me in love and mustering every ounce of energy to keep me moving is my precious wife, Pastor Mabel Odigie and of course, by our side, are three very loving and understanding children (Praise, Honor and Favor) both cheering us and bearing long with us in this tough undertaking called life. You are my earthly treasure and I can't wait to share your noisy neighborhood in Heaven.

Finally, to my powerful editing team for these series, my most profound thanks. Ms. Nadine Thomas who did initial transcribing; my daughters Omolara Olutunbi and Praise Odigie for great editing work on this book. Further professional editing was done by Pastor Gbenga Showumi, Ola Aboderin and Rosanda Richardson. You have all labored so hard, thank you. The author accepts responsibility for any observable errors and welcome your feedback.

CONTENTS

PREFACE

For many believers in Christ, addressing the myriad of internal conflicts, endless struggles, and contradictions that confront them daily, definitely require spiritual grit and determination. There is also a need to lift spiritual curtains and expose the secret layers of hidden demonic contaminations tucked away in a remote past of generational demonic influences and corruptions.
Hidden demonic covenants, curses, and a laundry list of self-inflicted wounds resulting from inappropriate interactions with controlling territorial demonic powers through ignorance and carelessness must be uncovered and cleared out.

To be sure, the ability to break free and live a meaningful, productive and fulfilling life calls for addressing critical issues in deliverance and aggressive warfare. Unfortunately, large sections of the Body of Christ are burdened with little understanding of effective deliverance training, and the devil's business thrives through ignorance. This needless darkness has proven to be problematic, leaving many genuine believers stuck at the crossroads of unidentified conflicts, delays, painful losses, and frustrations

The Word of God declares, "My people are destroyed for lack of knowledge" (Hosea 4:6). The Holy Spirit, writing through the

Apostle Paul, admonishes us to be abreast of Satan's devices:

"Lest Satan should get an advantage of us: for we are not ignorant of his devices" (2 Corinthians 2:11).

There is indeed much to thank God for in Deliverance Ministry today. However, much of the practice of deliverance ministry in this generation on closer observation seem deficient of real sound scriptural foundation. Just the other day, I heard a well-meaning and respectable Deliverance Minister define Deliverance as the act of casting out devils. This individual is a true laborer in the kingdom but his incomplete understanding of the operational definition of deliverance like many other well-meaning servants of God engenders serious problems as it sets out on a faulty premise.

If we embark on a journey without knowing where we are headed, how can we know for sure that we have reached our destination ultimately? While the process of deliverance entails casting out of demons, it is far more than that; you cannot cast out sin and while we are commanded to mortify the flesh, we can neither cast out the flesh nor the world we live in and these all impact on our deliverance from day to day.

The Preaching of deliverance is prevalent and the true teaching of deliverance is scarce and much limited in scope. What is the implication of this? While preaching can warn and motivate a desire for change of outcomes, it is sound teaching in all wisdom that can impart the actual know how to secure those desirable outcomes.

This is why every believer must be armed with adequate knowledge of the principles, purposes, and processes of total deliverance from the works of the devil. What Christ purchased for us with His Blood is total freedom from everything that is contrary to God's desire for our lives. And until this is achieved, no true believer must relent.

It is in furtherance of this goal of absolute freedom in Christ that this three-volume book has been written. This first volume dwells on the meaning, necessity and ramifications of deliverance, while the other two build on this foundation to explore other crucial issues and answer nagging questions on this very important subject. I expect that this book will be used by deliverance workers, spiritual warfare workers, and ministers of the gospel to help them really understand the subject in depth.

It is my prayer that, as you read, you will experience Spirit-inspired enlightenment that will position you for total emancipation from every bondage and limitation.

Chapter one

MY DYSFUNCTIONAL EARLY YEARS

I was born into a domestic war zone. My father had five wives and twenty-eight biological children. Because of this complicated polygamous setup, my father existed for all of his children but each mother existed only for hers. Distrust ruled the household. Each woman went to desperate measures to sustain herself, and sought out whatever local help was available in order to secure the survival of her children. And because the main sources of help they could access were demonic, witchcraft activity was inevitable. When my mother was pregnant with me, local witches in the area visited her and demanded for my life. According to my mother, they visited physically and quietly informed her that she was pregnant with a male child and they gave her the option to either surrender me to them or she would not be able to have another child. She opted to keep me and so, I became her last born.

As I grew up closely with my mother, I came to understand that she was involved in a marine-based religion; that is, she believed that she originated from a river spirit and raised an altar in our home to the marine goddess. My father himself was a medium, which I later realized was founded in a deep relationship with ancestral powers and the Leviathan spirit. As a child, I was often in my mother's company as she consulted with and patronized various traditional witch-doctors. The paraphernalia of witchcraft and their semi-prophetic ability left an outstanding impression on my young mind.

At a very early stage in life I was introduced to sexual activities which opened the doorway for Satan to strengthen his hold on my life. Though I was fascinated by the more appealing faith of Christianity, my attempts to practice it were to no avail. I did not understand who Jesus was, and I certainly was not saved.

In 1975, my family (that is, my mother and her children) underwent a severe crisis that pushed my mother to join a syncretic movement called Celestial Church of Christ. It was a church that mingled biblical truths with practices bordering on the occult. This new form of worship was easy to transition to, as the same spirits that were active in our traditional occult practice and rituals were very active in the celestial church movement experience (i.e. the predictive tongue and the Seeing Eye that flows from Leviathan involvement and marine spirits).

My mother joined the movement in 1975, bringing all her children on board and going further to establish branches of the movement in our family, and neighboring villages. This was where I called church until 1984 when I got saved through an encounter with the Lord Jesus. Before then, however, my entire life had come to revolve around Women, booze, and parties. I had reached a point where I decided that Christianity was not for me – not because Christianity was not valid, but because as a young man, I had become so entrenched in sexual perversion and felt helpless. Since I knew I couldn't combine wayward living with the tenets of Christianity, I let go of Christianity.

I would jokingly tell my friends back in those days: "I will have fun now and go to hell later." Once I made that decision, I gave into a riotous life. I partied and drank excessively anywhere the opportunity presented itself; and I would argue with anyone who dared to preach to me about Jesus Christ.

On February 28, 1984, at about 10:30 p.m. at the University of Calabar, Hall 3, Room One, (in Nigeria) I was preparing to go to a party in town with my friend, Chris Morris, when I overheard two young men talking about Jesus. I went over to argue with them as was my habit, mainly to prove to them that they did not know what they were saying. In the course of the argument, one of the young men, Lambert Ibe, dropped on his knees, looked me straight in the eye and started sobbing sorrowfully. That made an impression on me.

I remember thinking to myself, "Why is this man crying for me, as if I am dead?" The second young man, Tony Onawakpo, whom I later regarded as my spiritual father, looked straight into my eyes and asked me, "Patrick, why don't you repent?" Those words went through me. I wanted to argue but I could not. For the first time I found myself speaking from my heart, saying, "Yes, I know that Jesus is true; I know that the salvation experience is real, but I do not want to flatter myself because I know that I am incapable of sustaining a relationship with the Lord."

I imagined that my previous foray into "church" was equal to true

Christianity and I thought that since I was frequently running after women, there was no way of sustaining that kind of relationship without offending God. I said to the young man: "Imagine that you commit a crime and go before the judge who then sets you free. You commit more crimes, and you are brought before the same judge again and he sets you free. Imagine that you keep coming and going like that for a season, but after a given point in time, you realize that you are not able to use the freedom." I told him I was better off as I was, and Jesus would be better off if I did not come to Him because I would frequently go back and break His heart.

"Patrick," Tony said to me, "The Bible says that we as human beings must forgive one another seventy times seven. That is, if an individual offends you 490 times, keep forgiving. If God can ask that kind of standard from mere humans, will He Himself not forgive you so many more times, provided that right now you are truly repentant and sorry?" That went through me again. It was as if I could literally see the Father, Son and Holy Spirit right there saying, "If you are prepared to repent now, your sins will be forgiven."

At that moment, I thought about the countless women in my life. I thought about the booze, I thought about the parties, and the words that came out of my mouth were "I cannot stand." Everything in me wanted me to say yes but I knew I could not stand. I started to turn away and leave, but as I turned, my face connected with a poster on the wall. It was a poster of Jesus, with His bruised, battered, and bloodied Body. As my attention fell on that poster I was arrested. I could not move. For the first time, the piece of paper and drawing became meaningful to me. That was the Almighty God who loved me and was stripped naked on that wood. As I looked at it, I could not turn away. I dropped on my knees, pointed at the poster and asked, "God, did you do that for me? Did you do that for me?"

Suddenly, the poster transformed and it was as if I was transported back in time, seeing Jesus on the Cross going through the horrors. He spoke to me, saying, "Patrick, not only did I do this for you, I did it without saying one word in My defense because I knew you could not stand on your own. All you have to do is to look at this love and say you do not want it, and I will not bother you again. But remember, I did this without saying one word in My defense knowing that you could not stand on your own strength. Do you still say you cannot stand?" Somehow, a voice within me, and in spite of me, said "Lord, I can stand". I fell on my face, weeping, sobbing over my sins, the life I had lived: my selfishness, my rottenness, the corruption.

When I got up, two and half hours later, a few things happened. My friend with whom I was going to the party got angry and left. The Christians surrounded me and were jubilating, singing joyfully to the Lord. As I wanted to get up, the power of God hit me and I fell back. It was as if something was dissolving in my heart, and a movie of my life was passing by me. I felt so sorry for all that I had done. Then I was inflated with love for God. It was such deep love that filled me completely.

When I finally got up, a sense of peace and a new tenderness and love for God overwhelmed me. I got scared because I was reflecting on how I had wasted my life chasing shadows, not knowing that this was the real deal. Now that I had experienced it, I feared that I might wake up in the morning and find out it was a mere dream and I so badly wanted it to be for real. I stayed awake throughout that night. The following morning I was the first to arrive at the Protestant chapel.

That experience marked a dramatic turnaround in my life. I did not have to struggle to live a righteous life. All the women, all the booze, all the parties were instantly gone. I was saved, I was born again, I was happy in my Savior. Old things had passed away; all things had become new. I was set free by the Son of God and I was free indeed.

Indeed? Well, at least, for a season I enjoyed unprecedented peace and love for the Lord. I would stay in my little corner, looking at my little poster that said "Smile, Jesus Loves You". I skipped sleep many nights; I was so joyful that I just wanted to sing the praises of my Savior and Lord. In fact, my salvation caused a stir in the university because the people I used to hang out with immediately named me a fanatic, and the Christian community nicknamed me 'Holy Ghost Brother'.

Chapter Two

MY INTRODUCTION INTO DELIVERANCE

The Lord is very effective as a Shepherd. Psalms 78:70-72 shows us this truth:

"He chose David also his servant, and took him from the sheepfolds: From following the ewes' great with young he brought him to feed Jacob his people, and Israel his inheritance. So he fed them according to the integrity of his heart; and guided them by the skillfulness of his hands."

Here, the Lord is represented as David; that's why it says that He called David out to feed His inheritance, Jacob, and to lead His people Israel. And He fed them according to the integrity of His heart and guided them by the skillfulness of His hands.

Two powerful attributes of the Lord are portrayed here. He has complete integrity. In His integrity, He is thoroughly committed to us to the point of giving His life for ours. The Lord is also very skillful as a Shepherd. He knows how to guide each one of us. He does not throw everything at us at once.

Following my conversion, I spent some time basking in the euphoria of my newfound faith. I busied myself with writing gospel songs. I was on fire for God. You would have had to be in my situation to know the joy I felt at being free from the grip of sin, which, in my case, was sexual perversion. My life had been so perverted that I would have a girlfriend and would go to bed with her sister, and with her friend. I would pick up prostitutes by the wayside, and supplement with masturbation. I would go to bed with a girl knowing that she was not faithful to me but would still sleep with her. So, just knowing that I was free from sexual bondage was a most beautiful experience for me.

I had thought that was all. Quite frankly, I poured myself completely into Christianity. (This is expected of every true believer, anyway). I acquired every faith material I could lay hands on, not minding the cost. I had been used to spending lots of money on booze and women; but this time I was buying Bibles and all kinds of faith materials. I was growing rapidly in the faith. Within the first six months of my salvation experience, one would have thought that I had been a Christian for years. I was like an ordained minister, due to the knowledge of the Word of God I had acquired just by zealously loving the Lord.

But, then, some things began to happen.

EMBARASSING DREAM EXPERIENCE

The first was a bizarre dream I had, which I had wanted to forget very quickly. In this experience, I saw this huge bird, like a vulture, having sex with me. Quite disturbingly, I was really into it, and had all the feelings that go with such acts. I woke up feeling very shocked and embarrassed. As I said, it was an experience I had wanted to forget quickly, but it left a mark in my mind.

On another occasion, my friend and I had gone to minister Holy Spirit baptism to a fellow sister. As we were speaking in tongues, with our hands on her head, she suddenly slumped and began to foam at the mouth and twist like a snake. I beckoned to my friend and said, "This is a demon. We did not prepare for this. The Lord had told us to fast today but we did not fast. The Bible says this kind does not go out but by prayer and fasting, but we did not fast." I was quickly talking my friend and myself out of faith while the sister was on the ground twisting.

But the Lord has a sense of humor. At that point, the demon manifesting spoke through the sister and said, "Lucifer, help me! Lucifer, help me!" That caused us to roar back to life. Really? Was the demon calling Lucifer right where God the Father, the Son and the Holy Ghost were? We went ahead and cast out the devil. So, right there, Brother Patrick cast out his first demon! But I soon forgot about the incident and continued to enjoy my newfound faith in God.

However, not long after this, I was on summer holiday and visited my village. As I was walking through a bushy area, I thought I heard some people praying in the bush. I was curious and went closer, only to find two young men praying for another young man. They belonged to a particular Pentecostal church. I asked them why they were praying for him in the bush and they replied that they were conducting deliverance and that two snails had already left and there was another one in there. That sounded very bizarre to me. Snails? I thought those young men just wanted to give Christianity a bad rap; so I stopped them and sent them away. They obeyed me and left, but now I believe that that encounter was one of the first attempts the Lord had made to introduce me into deliverance ministry but I was not ready for it.

The next experience would be later on, when I read a book written by the late Victoria Eto, titled, The Forces of Darkness. It was scary. The book was an exposition on Ephesians 6, outlining in detail the structure of Satan's kingdom, namely, principalities, powers, rulers of darkness and spiritual wickedness in high places – and the powers that go with each. She was someone who had previously served Satan and was at one point in bed with Lucifer, and so had inside information into his kingdom. The book frightened me, so I put it aside.

After completing my first degree, the Lord led me to the northern part of Nigeria, which is predominantly Muslim, for my National Youth Service program. There, I led the Christian Youth Corps' Fellowship as the Prayer Secretary. I would fast and pray often at night. Within this period, I had some bizarre experiences. Often, when I interceded in the place of prayer, my spirit would be transported to pray in the spirit realm. On one of these occasions, as I prayed, the Holy Spirit transported me to a spiritual prison where people were in shackles. In this spiritual prison, Christians were being defiled, and all kinds of things bordering on satanic pollutions went on. One of the leaders of that satanic prison tried to get me compromised; but as I resisted, they threw me down and I was soon back in my body, still praying.

While at the Christian Youth Corps' Fellowship, the power of God was strong at our meetings. People were being delivered. I was just now being introduced into deliverance. I had a lot of impact there, but the light began to flash in my own spirit that I needed help. Suddenly, the sickness that I used to have as a child resurfaced. I was frequently having recurring episodes of fever, which were becoming protracted and interminable.

My old habits of quarrelling and anger were also fast coming back. We would have quarrels and fights at the executive meetings of the Christian Youth Corps Fellowship. On top of that, I would continue to have bizarre dreams. I knew I was in trouble and that I needed help. But where would I find it? This was when I remembered the deliverance book I had read (The Forces of Darkness). I asked about the author and was told that a branch of her ministry was located some 500 miles away from my station. I was serving in Maiduguri and the ministry was in Makurdi, all in Northern Nigeria.

At the end of the month, when I got my paycheck, I travelled down to Makurdi to seek my deliverance. My struggle for freedom intensified on the trip. Public transportation in those days were often overloaded, and it so happened that a young woman whom I had never met before sat by me on this trip. She threw her leg over mine and I did not even make the least effort to resist. Instead, I was quietly enjoying the warm contact. I knew I was in deep trouble. Old habits and desires were making a comeback. However, in wisdom, I did not tell her who I was or where I was going. I did not give her any information about myself or ask anything of her. I was just waiting to disembark from the vehicle to go and get help. When we disembarked, I went and traced the ministry in a hurry.

MY DELIVERANCE COUNSELING AND CLEANSING

When I got to my destination, the man of God I met there was used of the Lord to open the proverbial "Pandora's Box" of my life. He counseled me thoroughly. That counseling was the most probing interrogation of my life to date. All the rotten details of my past life, which I thought were no longer relevant being then a born again Christian – he dug them all up and wrote them down. Thereafter, he formed a prayer list and assigned two young men to pray for me.

I was disgusted when I saw those assigned to pray for me. What could such young men know? I was like Naaman, the Syrian, in the Bible story. I was so determined not to let them touch me. They, apparently, sensed my pride and did not try to touch me. They called me aside and prayed a very simple prayer, pleading the Blood of Jesus. They still did not touch me, but as they were pleading the Blood of Jesus, it was as if something hit me. I felt as if I was under anesthesia. I felt dizzy and began to foam at the mouth. At the same time, I was coughing up phlegm.

For one hour, I could not stop bringing up these things as these simple young men prayed. At the end of the prayer, I felt washed from within. It was as if I had been scrubbed from within. I felt clean, I felt pure. I asked, "Do you guys have any books on this thing?" They brought three books written by the leader of the ministry. They were entitled, The Forces of Darkness; How I Served Satan Until Jesus Delivered Me (which is a testimony book); and Exposition on Water Spirits. I read all of them within one week and went into fasting as I desperately wanted to know more about this phenomenon.

This is what launched my deliverance ministry. Soon after this experience, I went straight ahead into helping other people. Every other thing that happened, all the crises that were to follow—

indeed the warfare that was to follow were intense and severe – but the Lord trained and sustained me. This was how I entered into deliverance ministry in 1985 to this present day.

Chapter Three

WHAT IS DELIVERANCE?

Deliverance is the action of being rescued or set free; the act of delivering or the condition of being delivered. It means liberation, release, delivery, discharge, rescue, emancipation, salvation or bail out (Oxford Dictionary).

The following Scripture verses reveal some useful insights into what deliverance actually entails.

"But upon mount Zion shall be deliverance, and there shall be holiness; and the house of Jacob shall possess their possessions. And the house of Jacob shall be a fire, and the house of Joseph a flame, and the house of Esau for stubble, and they shall kindle in them, and devour them; and there shall not be any remaining of the house of Esau; for the LORD hath spoken it. And saviors shall come up on mount Zion to judge the mount of Esau; and the kingdom shall be the LORD's." (Obadiah 1:17, 18, 21).

Deliverance is total liberation and freedom from factors and agents that hinder or seek to hinder a man or a woman from enjoying the full benefits of their covenant relationship with God in Christ Jesus.(late Victoria Eto with my emphasis on the covenant dimension)..2 In other words, deliverance is a focused subject, predicated upon a covenant. I say focused in the sense that an individual seeker cannot benefit from the true experience of deliverance without embracing a committed relationship with the true and living God who alone delivers. Some people are deceived into thinking that they can just use God to resolve their issues and move on to live as they wish; but true deliverance entails committing to God in a covenant relationship, and that is freedom indeed. God will not deliver, except an individual takes hold of His covenant. Similarly, the devil cannot bind anyone, except there is some sort of covenant. The enemy actively seeks to bring people consciously or unconsciously into different types of binding covenant relationships, whereby he can exploit, oppress, suppress, defraud, kill, and destroy them. But for an individual to experience true deliverance, they have to take hold of God's covenant.

The entire Bible itself is, broadly speaking, divided into two covenants, called the Old Covenant (first covenant between Jehovah God and the nation of Israel) and the New Covenant (offered to the whole world through the sacrifice of our Lord Jesus Christ). The revelation of covenants in the Scriptures is both profound and progressive but the consummation of all and by far the most powerful covenant is that between the Father and the Son on behalf all mankind. This is referred to as the "Blood of the Everlasting Covenant." Hebrews 13:20 speaks of this:

"Now the God of peace that brought again from the dead our Lord Jesus, that great shepherd of the sheep, through the blood of the everlasting covenant."

In other words, in eternity past, God saw that man would fall from grace and become a victim of crafty and wicked spirits; therefore He prepared a covenant before laying the foundation of the earth. That is why the Bible says in Revelation 13:8 that the Lord Jesus Christ is the Lamb of God slain from the foundation of the earth. In other words, Calvary, even though a reality some 2000 years ago, is nevertheless a manifestation of a divine reality in eternity past. The only valid way for a man and woman to experience true freedom, is to enter into this covenant that God the Father had with the Son, which was consummated on Calvary through the death, burial, and resurrection of our Lord Jesus Christ.

"If we cast out a demon from an individual, we have not delivered him or her as yet. We have only given the person temporary relief."

BEYOND CASTING OUT OF DEMONS

When dealing with the subject of deliverance, people mostly focus on getting rid of demons. This is basic; but getting rid of demons is not in itself deliverance. If we cast out a demon from an individual, we have not delivered him or her as yet. We have only given the person temporary relief. True deliverance deals with the factors that actually validate and empower the enemy's presence in the life of an individual. Such factors include sin, the flesh, and worldliness.

There are many doorways that the enemy exploits in order to sneak into people's lives. These will be dealt with in a later part of the book. It must however be emphasized that when the enemy has gained entrance into an individual, he doesn't come to play. He busies himself reproducing his evil nature in the character of the oppressed person. This is why demonic intentions or manifestations are often hidden behind exaggerated behavior of the flesh in certain aspects of the human soul or personality.

When it comes to effective deliverance, you have to address the flesh also. You cannot cast out the flesh even though you can cast out demons. You also cannot cast out sin. Sin is transgression against God, and it is what gives the enemy legitimacy. Anything that is not in agreement with God is sin, and sin requires repentance. Where there is repentance of sin and denial or crucifixion of the flesh, the authority of the Holy Spirit will become available to force out the devil and to keep him out of the individual. This is what I mean by dealing with factors in addition to casting out the demon spirits.

WHERE CAN WE FIND TRUE DELIVERANCE?

Again, Obadiah 1:17 says, "Upon Mount Zion there shall be deliverance." Where do we find deliverance? It is upon Mount Zion. Mount Zion refers to the presence of God's Holy Spirit and power. Why do I say this? There are two opposing kingdoms – the Kingdom of God and the kingdom of Satan. Man is at the center or focus of these two kingdoms. When the power of God confronts the power of the enemy, we immediately see that which had been hidden begin to come to the surface. Mount Zion refers to God's stronghold, God's power-base, and it is activated when true believers in Jesus Christ gather together in true fellowship or worship.

There is also a historical side to this. In the time of King David of Israel, the people had been living in the Promised Land without actually possessing the full inheritance. When the territory of Canaan was conquered and divided by Joshua, there were pockets of places within the Promised Land which were still under the enemies' occupation. These were strongholds that had not yet been overthrown. One of such places was Jerusalem, inhabited by the Jebusites. They were so strong and the city so fortified that they had thought nobody could assail them. When David's generals received the mandate to take over territories within the Promised Land, the Jebusites boasted and said, "Look, we do not need to have able-bodied men to guard our cities, even our lame and blind are enough to ward you off because our gates are so fortified that nobody can penetrate anyway."

However, David challenged his mighty men to break through and conquer the city. Thereafter, David reconstructed it and made it his own stronghold. So Zion became the power-base of the capital in Jerusalem where he ruled physically.

"And the king and his men went to Jerusalem unto the Jebusites, the inhabitants of the land: which spake unto David, saying, Except thou take away the blind and the lame, thou shalt not come in hither: thinking, David cannot come in hither. Nevertheless David took the strong hold of Zion: the same is the city of David. And David said on that day, Whosoever getteth up to the gutter, and smiteth the Jebusites, and the lame and the blind, that are hated of David's soul, he shall be chief and captain. Wherefore they said, the blind and the lame shall not come into the house. So David dwelt in the fort, and called it the city of David. And David built roundabout from Millo and inward. And

David went on, and grew great, and the LORD God of hosts was with him." (2 Samuel 5: 6-10).

What is true physically is also true spiritually. There is a spiritual Zion. The Bible tells us about the spiritual Zion in Hebrews 12:22-24. We see the constituents of the spiritual Zion, which the Bible tells us are the company of innumerable angels, the church of the firstborn whose names are written in heaven, the presence of God the Father as the Judge of All, the presence of the Lamb of God, as the mediator between God and man, and the blood of sprinkling that speaks better things.

So, we have the blood of the Lamb, which is the legal basis, the legal ground, on which God delivers; we have the firepower of God's Holy Spirit that compels compliance and obedience from the enemy; we have the angels, innumerable ones the Bible says, that cannot be numbered.

TWO KINGDOMS AT WAR

So we immediately see that any time there is confrontation, two kingdoms are at war – one is weak and the other is strong. (Derek Prince notes of Spiritual Warfare) The stronger one is the Kingdom of Jesus Christ, of course. As strong as Satan's kingdom may pretend to be, before the power of the Living God, it is a very weak kingdom. That becomes quickly visible when there is a confrontation. This is why Satan hates deliverance. It brings into the open things he would rather keep secret; besides, it reveals the superiority of the firepower and the Kingdom of our Lord Jesus Christ over his. So, the will to deliver, the power to deliver, the covenant that conveys the deliverance, the legal grounds of the Blood of Jesus – all of these God has provided and man can access them through faith in the Lord Jesus Christ.

"There is no point in trying to minister deliverance to a man or a woman who is not prepared to surrender to the Lordship of Jesus Christ."

Unless people are willing to surrender to the authority of the Lord Jesus Christ, they really cannot be delivered. There is no point in trying to minister deliverance to a man or a woman who is not prepared to surrender to the Lordship of Jesus Christ. The Scripture tells us that such cases will lead to even more complications. We understand from Matthew 12:43-45 that when an unclean spirit is gone out of a man, it goes about seeking rest and, finding none, it says, "I will go back to my house where I was evicted." And it goes back and gets seven more wicked spirits and they invade that man or woman and the state of that person is worse than at the beginning.

This is to say that unless somebody is prepared to renounce the devil and submit to the Lordship of Jesus Christ, any attempt to minister deliverance to such an individual will be both a waste of time and a complication of an already existing bad situation.

THE FIRST LEVEL OF DELIVERANCE

The first level of deliverance is to surrender to the Lordship of Jesus Christ. In fact, I often say you cannot deliver somebody who is not already delivered. In other words, the basis on which you and I, as deliverance ministers, can administer deliverance to an individual is that they are already delivered or already under the covenant of Jesus Christ.

Colossians 1:13 says, that we have redemption through the Blood of Jesus, having been translated by the Father from under the dominion of the kingdom of Satan and darkness, into the Kingdom of His dear Son. In other words, by receiving Jesus Christ, we enter into the benefit of divine translation. We are immediately removed from under the rule, dominion, and government of Satan, and grafted into the rule and government of the Lord Jesus Christ.

"By the force of translation... every act of aggression or oppression by the devil becomes illegal and therefore can be judged and destroyed through application of the Word of God and the power of the Holy Spirit in deliverance ministration."

By the force of translation, we are moved from the state of the fallen man, past the fallen angels, even past the elect angels, and grafted into God's intimate family as sons and daughters of the Living God. By reason of this, every act of aggression or oppression by the devil becomes illegal and therefore can be judged and destroyed through application of the Word of God and the power of the Holy Spirit in deliverance ministration.

PROPHETIC INSIGHT

Still in Obadiah 1:17-18; it says "and there shall be holiness and the sons of Jacob shall possess their possessions." Immediately, we begin to see that deliverance should lead to something; it should lead to holiness. Another word for holiness is "wholeness" or "completeness." Everything and anything in your life and in my life that makes us not to feel whole or complete, the power of the Holy Spirit wants to apply the Blood of Jesus and deal with that fragmentation in order to bring wholeness or completeness or holiness in us.

Not only does deliverance lead to holiness or completeness, the Bible says also "the sons of Jacob shall possess their possessions." In other words, deliverance is one of God's methods of transmitting the benefits of our inheritance in Christ to us as believers. Your deliverance is directly related to your inheritance. You have a certain inheritance in God and the enemy wants to seize this. He is an aggressor, a ruthless, devious one, who does not play fair. That is why he has to be compelled by the power of God to yield his ground.

For male, female, old, young, new converts, ministers of the gospel – anything that infringes upon your inheritance is calling for divine attention and retribution. It means that what Jesus died to give you, the enemy wants to steal from you. You have to go after the enemy, eyeball to eyeball, shoulder to shoulder, and cut him down. We have a right to possess our possessions in God. You must be really "angry" about any gap in your life, any lack of fulfillment in your life, any sickness in your life, any oppression in your life, and in your family. You must be so angry and go to war to correct the situation.

The enemy cannot be allowed to get away with his illegality. It is illegal for a blood-bought child of God to live under satanic oppression. Something more that is said in this beautiful prophetic chapter in Obadiah is, "and the house of Jacob shall be fire, and the house of Joseph a flame, and the house of Esau for stubble, and they shall kindle together and there shall not be any remaining of the house of Esau". What is it saying?

"You have to go after the enemy eyeball to eyeball, shoulder to shoulder, and cut him down."

THE THREE CATEGORIES OF PEOPLE IN CHURCH

First, the passage mentions the House of Jacob. What is the House of Jacob? Jacob is the one with a promise; the covenanted child. He had done nothing of his own holiness or righteousness; neither have you, but by the fact that you are in Christ Jesus, you are in covenant with the Almighty God. All that Jesus is, all that He paid for, all that is available to Him is available to you. So, in Christ Jesus, we are a type of the sons of Jacob.

Why the emphasis on Jacob? This is very interesting. God is a God of redemption. Jacob means "the tricky one," "the supplanter." In other words, he had the promise of God and was covered by covenant but he was not very straight. And that is how many of us are. In certain aspects of our lives, we are still a work-in-progress. There are struggles; there are fleshly, carnal, and sinful behaviors. I am not excusing that, but I am simply saying that whatever contradictions there are in the character of a child of God cannot invalidate the covenant. There is still a covenant, and that covenant stands.

Jacob was the one who had the promise but often did things his own way. God promised to cover him with fire. Fire burns. Thank God for the fire of the Holy Spirit. It burns wickedness; it burns the devil, but the same fire preserves the believer in Christ Jesus. The fire of God is in the house of the Lord, covering the children of God and protecting them. When the Israelites left Egypt, God covered them with a pillar of cloud by day and a pillar of fire by night.

In the church of the living God today, people are at various levels of grace that they are walking in. However, if you are an authentic member of the Body of Christ, who still believes in Jesus Christ, you are covered by that fire. It says, "the house of Jacob shall be fire". Fire burns sin from our lives. It burns circumstances that the enemy can try to use to destroy us.

"Contradictions… in the character of a child of God cannot invalidate the covenant."

I want to emphasize that this is very wonderful and meaningful because as Jacob departed from his uncle, Laban, God confronted him on the way. He wrestled with God, and the Bible says God turned his name from Jacob to Israel, meaning he was no longer a cheat but a prince of God, having power with God and power with man. In that encounter, God changed his name and said to him, "Your name shall no more be called Jacob but Israel."

Hundreds of years later, God confronted Moses in the burning bush in the Sinai wilderness and commissioned him to go to Egypt. Moses wanted to know from God what to say to Israel in Egypt. God told Him:

> *"I AM THAT I AM… Thus shalt thou say unto the children of Israel, The Lord God of your fathers, the God of Abraham, the God of Isaac, and the God of Jacob, hath sent me unto you: this is my name for ever, and this is my memorial unto all generations" (Exodus 3:14-15).*

Notice that God did not say 'the God of Israel' but instead, the God of Jacob; amazing! He is still the God of Abraham, God of Isaac, and God of Jacob. The mere fact that God identifies himself as the God of Jacob is meaningful and liberating to the soul. Jacob is the imperfect one but covered by a perfect God with a covenant relationship. This means even though we are still a work in progress in many respect, the devil cannot lay hold on us because we are covered with the blood covenant God has with the Lord Jesus Christ.

So, are you a child of God today in the house of the Lord, and you find that you are still a work-in-progress and the enemy is trying to lie to you, suggesting to you that, based upon certain things in your life, he has to have you under oppression? I want to say to you, no way! That is not the gospel.

Of course, God does not want us to continue in sin so that grace may abound. No! We have been delivered from the power of sin. You are not under the law, you are definitely under grace. You are covered by the fire of God. If you were around me, I would kick out that devil from you. I wouldn't waste any time; I wouldn't struggle with you because I stand under the authority of God to kick that devil out of your life. You deserve to be free. That is the Word of God.

THE ANOINTING VERSUS THE GLORY
(THE HOUSE OF JOSEPH)

Obadiah says that the House of Joseph shall be for a flame. What is the difference between fire and flame? Fire burns but flame cuts. Superior blue flame will cut iron. Flame speaks of the glory of God. The House of Joseph here is a reference to those within the Body of Christ who dare to pay the price of separation. Joseph was the separated one. He was separated from his brethren. The Bible says

"Let the blessing come 'on the head of Joseph, And on the crown of the head of him who was separate from his brothers,'" (Deuteronomy 33:16, NKJV).

Because Joseph was separated from his brethren, he brought the blessing to the rest. He presented them with posterity. I am saying prophetically also that God will raise up a people with the anointing of Joseph within the church of the Lord Jesus, who will embrace the authentic spirit of consecration, and they will stretch out before God and embrace the flame and the glory.

In the fire, the anointing functions; but in the flame the glory functions. What is the difference? God can anoint a man or woman who can have the Holy Ghost and fire, but does not go all the way, and the enemy can still function through their flesh. But in the glory, the flame, the enemy does not have any equipment to work with because in the glory God judges the flesh but then brings and unleashes a higher level of authority. So there are people who are consecrated; and you who are reading this book, you will be one of those vessels whom God will give the courage to love Him passionately, to go past the regular profession of Christianity; and to go deeper and more intimate with Him.

"The end of man is the beginning of the glory of God!"

You are going to seek God in fasting and in prayer. You are going to cry after Him. You want to be like Him, and get hold of Him. And guess what? It is going to happen. The flame will be upon you. I believe that the Lord Jesus best exemplifies this. From time to time, He moved in that glory and the enemy saw it, and demons were terrified and began to scream, "We know You, we know who You are, the Holy One of God, have You come to torment us before the time?"

That's the realm of glory. And where are the Josephs of this generation? I summon you to rise up. Rise up! Because God wants to use you on the earth today. In the anointing, the gifted man is in evidence; but in the glory, we come to the end of the man. The end of man is the beginning of the glory of God.

FASTING AND THE GLORY DIMENSION OF THE ANOINTING

The Lord spoke to me through a vision in December 2001. I was visiting the United Kingdom, fellowshipping with my esteemed friend, Pastor Jerome Obode, at the time. We enjoyed robust times of prayer and fasting at very fulfilling and productive levels during this visit. We were excited for more of the Lord and decided to proceed on a twenty-one day complete fast. The fasting barely got underway when I had a very telling trance.

In the vision, I saw the late Archbishop Benson Idahosa on a large podium, kneeling and with his hands on the floor at the same time. There was an empty chair by his side and, in the meantime, Pastor Enoch Adeboye of the Redeemed Christian Church of God came and sat on the empty chair across from the Archbishop. Suddenly, he placed his two feet over the Archbishop and in a seeming disrespectful manner pushed him out of the stage. Just then, my eyes were opened, while still wondering how the gentle Pastor could do that to the late Archbishop.

The Holy Spirit of God began to explain the meaning of the revelation to me. He said that the two men represented different phases of His program and move on the earth. According to the Holy Spirit, the late Archbishop represented the charismatic move, while Pastor Adeboye represented the glory move. In the charismatic move, He said, He anointed gifted men who attracted a large following to the Kingdom. The late Archbishop represented this and brought great respectability and appeal to the gospel. However, under the charismatic gift, anointed or gifted men can still be corrupted and bring the cause of the gospel into disrepute.

The glory move is very different, however. According to the Holy Spirit, "in the glory move, I don't need the gift of a man; instead, I kill the man. The end of man is the beginning of the glory of God."

In the charismatic move, the anointed man can still carry the flesh around and the devil will work with that to impose limitations, containments and corruption. In the glory move, the flesh is crucified and the enemy has no equipment with which to work. Fasting, according to God, is one of the instruments of death to the flesh. He used the anointed ministry of the late Archbishop Idahosa to pioneer the charismatic move in Nigeria but He is using the ministry of Pastor E.A. Adeboye to pioneer the glory move.

THE HOUSE OF ESAU

This is the third level or category of people (house) in the Church of God. This house is a bad one. It is called the House of Esau. Esau, in the Bible, is referred to as the profane one. The Bible says "Lest there be any fornicator, or profane person, as Esau, who for one morsel of meat sold his birthright" (Hebrews 12:16). It says further that, afterwards, when he would have inherited the blessing, he was rejected. He was rejected and he found no room for repentance even though he sought it carefully with tears.

The implication of this is that the choices we make are very important. Your choice today is shaping your tomorrow. It is affecting every person around you. It is affecting heaven, and it is even affecting time and eternity. Our choices are very important to God and man.

There are too many people today who play around. They give God sentimental or emotional commitments. But when it comes to time to really make decisions, they do not take the narrow road; they want the easy way out. They practice the kind of Christianity the devil does not respect. The Lord will not honor such because His desire for us is to be a committed people. So the house of Esau is the profane. And God says the fire of Jacob and the flame of Joseph shall combine and destroy profanity from the house. The Bible says, in fact, that there shall be none remaining of the house of Esau.

I am so glad that God is not going to leave us in this defeated and humiliated state of the Church. The anointing of God, the outpouring of God's Holy Spirit, will come upon the Body of the Lord, and a people will rise on the earth who will love God passionately. They will give God radical commitment and will do exploits. The devil does not stand a chance. They will demonstrate the complete defeat of the enemy as they move in their end-time authority of the sons of God and fulfill their ministry on the earth.

The Bible says finally in Obadiah 1:21,

> *"And saviors shall come up on mount Zion to judge the mount of Esau; and the kingdom shall be the LORD'S."*

Note that it doesn't say savior but saviors. It is plural. Here is what this means: God will anoint some consecrated men and women who will be radical and they will carry governmental authority. This is one thing that will be increasingly important as we press further into these end times. God is going to raise men and women, old and young, and release the government of the Lord Jesus upon them. They will experience governmental authority to judge profanity on the earth, to break curses, to undo burdens, and to release many into liberty; and I believe you and I are called to be a part of this beautiful army of the Lord Jesus Christ. Hallelujah! Thank you Lord.

Chapter Four

THE DELIVERANCE PROCESS

There is a clear deliverance process revealed in the Scriptures. What do I mean by deliverance process? It is the process whereby God, the Holy Spirit, brings a believing person from satanic bondage to actual liberty. There is a process whereby He does this work. I would like to reference this particular Scripture in Isaiah which depicts the whole anointing of deliverance:

> *"The Spirit of the Lord GOD is upon me; because the LORD hath anointed me to preach good tidings unto the meek; he hath sent me to bind up the brokenhearted, to proclaim liberty to the captives, and the opening of the prison to them that are bound; To proclaim the acceptable year of the LORD, and the day of vengeance of our God; to comfort all that mourn; To appoint unto them that mourn in Zion, to give unto them beauty for ashes, the oil of joy for mourning, the garment of praise for the spirit of heaviness; that they might be called trees of righteousness, the planting of the LORD, that he might be glorified" (Isaiah 61:1-3).*

What this passage is saying, if you look at it and break it down a little bit, is that the process of deliverance begins with hearing the gospel message and receiving it in faith. This is critical because as I said before, there are two kingdoms that are reaching out for the souls of men. One is the kingdom of darkness that wants to destroy our souls in stages through life and eternity, and the other is the Kingdom of God, which has the original blueprint for destiny fulfillment and actualization of the human soul.

Every human being born into this world is dead on arrival. This has been so since the fall of Adam except your Parents are believers in which case you are sanctified by their faith until you reach the age of accountability; but when you come into Jesus Christ, you move from death to life. Of course this raises the questions of what happens to all who die in their infancies. My response to that is that God is perfectly just and we can trust that he knows how to cover them.

However, even though you are now out of the grave, the influences, decorations (meaning satanic emblems) deposited by demons, and implants conferred on you, while in the grave in a tomb of sin within the devil's camp, need to be dealt with. The reason is that these are the tools he uses and will continue to want to use even after you are born again.

"Every human being born into this world is dead on arrival"

POINTS OF CONTACT

There is something in deliverance called the points of contact. These are things Satan has planted in your life. He uses them against you when you have moved over to the Kingdom of

Light. These are the things that people feel – the constraints, the limitations, and the demonic containments – that do not allow them to express themselves and be fulfilled in life. These challenges predispose the oppressed persons to seek answers. More detail on points of contact is provided in volume two of this series.

NEW DNA AND KINGDOM TRANSFER

In order to meaningfully address points of contact, a person first needs a kingdom change. That is why people must hear the Gospel, and the Bible calls it preaching the Gospel to the meek, or those who are poor in spirit; that is, those who are humble enough to accept the simple message of the Cross.

The first thing that happens is that you receive a kingdom transfer (Colossians 1:13), where you are transferred automatically from Satan's kingdom into the Kingdom of God, into the family of God. And there is also a blood transfusion in the spirit whereby the born again child of God actually receives God's DNA through the Blood or Life of the Lord Jesus Christ.

Sin is a spiritual thing in the nature of man. When someone carries the nature of the devil, being a sinner, they cannot cast Satan out of his property as it were; but when you come to Christ, there is a spiritual blood transfusion in the spirit and God's DNA becomes written into your system, and the life of God is given to you. You are then automatically transferred from Satan's kingdom. From this point, everything Satan does against you is actually illegal.

Being born again, being grafted into God's nature, is the first level of deliverance. The person who has not gained this level of deliverance has not yet begun the process. Anything the deliverance minister tries to do with such a person will only produce more confusion and more complications. That is why we find that a lot of people who go to deliverance meetings sometimes come out worse. It is putting the cart before the horse.

When people are born again, the next level in the deliverance process is counseling. It is referenced in Scripture as "binding up the brokenhearted" (Isaiah 61). Binding the brokenhearted requires skill. I hear people say there is nothing like deliverance ministry. I think that is a statement usually made in pride by an individual who does not fully understand what this ministry is all about. There is deliverance ministry. It is part of the Gospel. All are called to preach, but some people will be mandated by God to pay closer attention to certain aspects of the Gospel. We generally assume that we are called to preach the Bible. Nobody can preach the Bible. The Bible is a very big subject. God can give us a theme in the Bible and make us to specialize in that theme. Still, all of us, put together, are preaching the Gospel.

Deliverance is a valid part of God's Word, and God in His wisdom does call people to pay more particular attention to this ministry because it requires skill – more particularly when it has to do with binding up the brokenhearted. We call these people specialized, skillful spiritual counselors, who understand the nature of the human soul that has been violated by the wicked. People go through different levels of satanic violation, some as early as when they were in the womb, or in the formative years of their lives.

In the process of my involvement in the deliverance ministry for the past 30 years, I have found out that the enemy always makes a desperate move to sexually violate children by the age of five. That is one of the fastest ways to put demons in them. We find that when children are sexually violated at the age of five, six or seven, the demons gain access but remain largely dormant, waiting for the opportune moment. By the time the children reach their teenage years, the demons fill them with inordinate curiosity and get them to indulge in activities that open them up more to evil. Eventually, they end up struggling to find purpose and fulfillment all through life.

"People who carry invisible spiritual wounds are like a man at war within himself; so it requires counseling."

People who are damaged may be well-dressed and look nice, but they have contradictions in their lives that they don't understand. Some are trying to serve God but cannot seem to break loose from certain habits and cannot understand what is going on. The spirit of counsel is an anointing of God that functions in prophets and, to a great measure, in those who are called by God to work in the deliverance ministry.

Specialized, skillful deliverance counselors are trained individuals who should be able to help those who are violated or are going through demonic oppressions and bring them into liberty. This is done through introspective investigations of their past lives to uncover where their souls have been violated and scarred, or where demonic infestations and wounds in the spirit have occurred so that they can skillfully work with them to clean them out.

There are many people who carry invisible spiritual wounds in the soul, and because their soul is deeply violated and fragmented, they cannot seem to get things together. It is like a man at war within himself; so it requires counseling.

In most deliverance encounters, the battles are lost or won depending on the skillfulness of the person doing the initial counseling. We often want to jump to the action side and kick the devil out. The devil enjoys that because it really is not effective. Yes, we will see the power of God and the weakness of demons. We probably get excited and carried away when we see the power of the Holy Spirit in action, knocking people down, with demons crying out and fleeing. But the ultimate goal is to ensure that the demons do not return.

To ensure that demons never return, the first step, as I pointed out earlier, is for the person to be born again. The next most important step is effective counseling and that is what is called binding up the brokenhearted. You counsel the individual and probe deeply into their lives to find out what has really happened in the course of their lives. What are the things that have violated them? What activities, associations and interactions have they been involved in? Sometimes it runs deep to include even their parents. It means that there may be things that they themselves don't know about – things that were done by their parents.

In some cultures, having a child is so significant that people go to all kinds of places to get one. When such a child is born, Satan already has a tag on them, and the demons are there to enforce the agreement that is on that child. The child is not even aware of it, and so the child goes through life and eventually comes to find out that there is something that is strange about him or her. Although this example is very prevalent in African countries, I have found out that this happens even in the Western world. I was reading a book by a deliverance minister in America many years ago and the main character in that book had an interesting story. The parents were poor and the child was born with some kind of disease condition and needed some help. A blood transfusion was done, the bills were paid for by an unknown benefactor, who turned out to be a satanic person, and the child was sold to the devil and the battle commenced in her life.

Satan is alive and well all over the world. His demons are active, his agents are active; it is just that when it comes to the Western world it is more sophisticated and rationalized, which really gives the devil a cover under which to function.

THE SPIRIT OF COUNSEL

The spirit of counsel is a major aspect of the anointing that was upon the Lord Jesus, the same anointing which we share. In the Scriptures, we see the seven-fold spirit upon the Lord Jesus Christ - the Spirit of the Lord, the Spirit of wisdom and understanding, the Spirit of counsel and might, the Spirit of knowledge and of the fear of the Lord (Isaiah 11:2).

It is instructive to note that in the above verse, counsel comes before might. Therefore, in conducting deliverance, before exercising might - which is to cast out the devil - we need counsel. This is how you can discover all that had happened; it is how you come to find out whether the individual you are ministering to has aided and given cover to the enemy to function in his or her own life. I emphasize this because I am doing this book as a kind of theoretical analysis to help people understand the nature of deliverance; that is, how deliverance really works because spiritual warfare and deliverance are a major part of God's end-time program on the earth. A lot of good is going on but, sorrowfully, too, a lot of misunderstanding, a lot of immaturity and a lot of confusion abound on the subject – the result of which is that sometimes the wonderful works of God are caricatured and the truth is left in contempt.

Essentially, the Spirit of counsel is part of what comes upon you as a worker in the kingdom to be able to sit with people and take an introspective journey into their lives and unearth the things that the enemy has done. That is why, sometimes, when I am doing deliverance for people, I do not want to jump into the prayer aspect. I try to put them in touch with the Lord and even recommend some days of fasting. Why? Because I want the Holy Spirit to meet with them and begin to signal some things in their lives.

People need to know that there is a deliverance process. Deliverance is not a magic wand where you just go to some kind of meeting and things are cast out of you. If you get something cheap, you will probably lose it very cheaply too. That is why most of what is done in deliverance is not sustained and people have to come back again and again, with deliverance delayed in a cycle of confusion and frustration.

"It is instructive to note that in the above verse, counsel comes before might. Therefore, in conducting deliverance – before exercising might, which is to cast out the devil – we need counsel."

It is important that we know how the deliverance process works, and a major part of it is the counseling or the binding of the brokenhearted. In fact, it is through the process of counseling that wounds in the soul are uncovered and deep inner healing and deep inner cleansing can take place.

I will come back to the subject of deep inner cleansing within the deliverance process a little later on. However, I cannot over-emphasize the area of counseling. The person desiring deliverance is first brought to the faith - they have to be willing to accept Jesus

Christ as the basis for starting; but then once we are ready to really go into deliverance proper, the next important step is counseling.

Binding up the brokenhearted is counseling – going into the deep issues of their personal lives, seeking the wisdom and insight of the Holy Spirit to unearth how these people came into bondage. What kind of spirit is functioning? How has that spirit reproduced its character in the individual? When bondage occurs, demons do not come into the life of people to play games or to have a vacation. They seek a home in the oppressed person; they have a destructive nature which they will exercise in the life of the individual and they have an evil character which they will also reproduce in the individual's life.

"It is through the process of counseling that wounds in the soul are uncovered and deep inner healing and deep inner cleansing can take place."

For effective deliverance to happen, the aforementioned must be followed. If not, you can eliminate the demon while his character or image is still inside the oppressed person. Eventually, the demon comes back and reoccupies. It is in counseling that we can show people what has happened; for example, the exaggerated aspect of their human character due to demonic corruption and the need to undergo crucifixion. It is like working with wounded people in a hospital and this is why not everybody can succeed here. It is not about power - even though power is required; it is so much more about skill, training and understanding how it works.

It is not merely running all over the place, knocking people down under the power of God and basically not caring about them. Our God wants to nurture His people back to health. He wants to bless them and break the curses on their lives. He wants to remove their wounds, heal them, make them whole and then they will be able to function in their true destiny.

BREAKING EVIL GRIPS

Another important component of the deliverance process after counseling is to literally apply the power of God and to clean out the individual. It is what I call the practical deliverance session.

During deliverance or cleaning out of an oppressed person, you must understand again that the ground for deliverance is the Blood. As I said earlier on in the definition, deliverance is based on the Blood covenant that God has with Jesus, which we have come into by faith. As you counsel people, you will need to put them in touch with the Lord, while being yourself very sensitive to the Lord. You are very likely to discover the root causes, hidden curses and demonic covenants, which can now be broken by the application of the Blood.

Satan's aggression, human rebellion, and the conditions that produce bondage can be brought under judgment and remedied by application of the precious Blood of Jesus Christ. Again, it is important that we understand that the Blood of Jesus is the legal ground on which God delivers. He said "when I see the Blood I will pass over you" (Exodus 12:13). The Blood of Jesus, validly applied, attracts the power and the presence of God.

There is also the firepower of the Holy Spirit. By reason of the anointing, the yoke becomes destroyed (Isaiah 10:27). The anointing of the Holy Spirit comes when the Blood is validly applied to the situation. The power of the Holy Spirit comes and breaks the bondage.

Understanding the deliverance process is vital to those who work in this area and want to see good things happen. We must understand that there are different types of cases and scenarios. I will deal more on this when I start to talk about why some deliverance cases seem to delay. It is a challenge in this area of ministry because we want to see quick results as it often happened with Jesus. This is wonderful. I believe in increase of grace. But I must say that if God has us patiently take one person through this process effectively, that is a lot. We should be looking at the human being who is suffering. We should also be looking at the fact that Jesus paid the price for people to be free. We should be patiently working to see people come to complete liberty.

"... we tend to counsel people in a way which can only be explained as teaching them how to cohabit successfully with their demons. This is ridiculous! You cannot counsel demons; you cast out demons!"

Casting out demons is an important part of the deliverance process. Atimes, we tend to counsel people in a way which can only be explained as teaching them how to cohabit successfully with "their" demons. This is ridiculous! You cannot counsel demons; you cast out demons! If they are there - you locate them in the counseling session; but, after that, the power needs to come in to clean the person out.

I will not go into details now on how to recognize when demons are coming out and how to know when they are gone - we will look at those details later on - though as part of the process of casting out demons, it is very important. This is the part of the process that people focus their attention upon. Even for those who are coming to seek deliverance, initially their whole focus is,

"I just want to get rid of the demon, get this thing out of me."

Well, it is one thing to kick a demon out, but it is another thing to keep it out. In order to effectively kick it out and keep it out, we have to understand how the process works. Everything, both the natural and the spiritual, has a process. People do not get pregnant today and deliver a baby tomorrow. It takes a nine-month period of gestation within which people can prepare for the coming of the baby. It is the same with deliverance. It is a process.

Now, the next thing, after you have kicked out the devil, is to keep him out. How do you do that? The person who has been delivered has to be taught the Word of God. This is a crucial one. Remember, in deliverance, we bring the anointing of God, the Spirit of Justice, to release judgment on the devil and to give relief to the oppressed. Once the oppressed is cleaned up, we should teach them to be filled with the power of God's Holy Spirit. But we must remember that God's Holy Spirit only bears witness to God's Holy Word. Therefore, a major part of the deliverance process is teaching and discipleship of people in the Word of God.

Sadly, this is currently one big failure of deliverance ministries. We just recycle stuff, talk more and more about how to be free, cast out devils, bind this and bind that, all of which only brings marginal success.

NO ALTERNATIVE TO GOD'S WORD

If people do not embrace the Word of God in their lives, they really cannot enjoy true freedom. Jesus was speaking to believers in the Book of John: "Then he said to some people who believed on Him" – see, they believed – "if ye continue in my word, then are ye my disciples indeed. And you shall know the truth and the truth shall make you free" (John 8:30-32). And when Jesus was restating His mission statement in Luke 4:18, He quoted Isaiah 61, saying, "…and recovering of sight to the blind".

Yes, the power of the Gospel can bring healing to blind people, but the worst form of blindness on earth today is ignorance of the Word of God. Progressive encounter of the revealed truth of God's Word brings people into various degrees of liberty. The more you know, the more you gain liberty; the more you know, the more your freedom increases. So, there is a need to know – to know the basics of our faith, to know the doctrines of sound faith.

"If people do not embrace the Word of God in their lives, they really cannot enjoy true freedom."

We are so quickly producing a generation of emotional Christians who are very much in touch with the social media but have little time for the Word of God; yet there can be no freedom without the Word of God. The Word of God is given by a loving God to us to restore our violated and fragmented soul. It is through the revelation of that Word of God that we come into harmony with God - our nature, which had been violated from one degree to the other, being reclaimed, restored, and reconciled to God. As we become one with Him, His peace settles in us and our heart is established with grace.

Nothing can replace the Word of God. In fact, deliverance is the execution of the Word of God against Satan's rebellion. If people who are seeking deliverance do not embrace the Word of God, or are not taught the Word of God and do not understand the centrality of the Word of God to their success, they cannot go very far. Satan will always be able to come around to steal, to kill, and to destroy them. James 4:7 says, "Submit yourselves therefore to God. Resist the devil, and he will flee from you."

How can you submit to a God you do not see? You can only submit to His Word. The Word of God is the same as God Himself. So when we submit to the Word, we become like Him, and Satan loses his hold. This point needs to be emphasized again and again. The failures that we see in deliverance ministry today are largely related to our inability to systematically train people in the Word of God.

There is an enemy out there. He is very much interested in our failure. But we do not have to fail because God has given us the tools to succeed. We can build our ministries around our gifts and anointing, but our gifts and our anointing only attract people to us. When people are attracted to us, the most they can do is to be like us; whereas, the Word of God will wean people from us and put them in touch with their eternal Creator.

The more people become like God, the further darkness will get away from them. The Bible says, "Looking unto Jesus, the author and finisher of our faith" (Hebrews 12:2). Seekers of deliverance cannot look unto Jesus if they do not know His Word. Yes, deliverance is real; warfare is real. But let us do it the right way. The Word of God is central and holds everything under creation together.

Once people embrace the Word of God, that Word goes deep and begins to correct satanic contradictions within them. Their scarred, disconnected, fractured nature begins to come together in wholeness. Then they will find out that they have inner peace and are unafraid. They can grow in love with God, for God and go ahead to fulfill their destiny. It takes a loving God and His Word to be strong enough to do exploits in this world.

THREE PHASES OF DELIVERANCE

Deliverance is in three phases. These include the past, the present, and the future. Let me explain it with these subheadings: (1) Faith in the Lord Jesus Christ, repentance towards God and initial counseling and casting out of residual demons; (2) Ongoing period of warfare, trainings and growth in the Word of God; and (3) Maturing in spiritual authority and growth in dominion

SALVATION AND INITIAL COUNSELLING/ DELIVERANCE

The first phase of deliverance is embracing saving faith in the Lord Jesus Christ and renunciation of evil covenants. When you give your life to Christ and come into that beauty of God's deliverance, you are automatically removed from under the dominion of darkness to the dominion of light. In other words, you have moved from under Satan's authority and brought into God's Kingdom. Satan can only function illegally against you at that point. That is the first level of deliverance.

SECOND PHASE AND INTENSE WARFARE

The second phase is related to what the Holy Spirit is doing every day in your life in the present sense. The Lord is busy at work in each of His children every single day. We must identify what it is that the Lord is doing, in order to meaningfully connect with it. This again is important because deliverance is not the work of a deliverance minister. He is a vessel being used by the Holy Spirit. This means that your deliverance is not limited to the church or the deliverance minister.

Most of your deliverance can, in fact, happen between you and God, if you simply submit to the divine process and recognize that it is the Holy Spirit at work in you. This will enable you to continue to work with the Holy Spirit, and He will be doing things in your life. In fact, one of the reasons people are so disconnected is that they cannot understand what the Lord is doing in their lives in a present sense. If you do not know what the Lord is doing in your life at the moment, you will become distracted by what the devil is doing against you.

To further understand deliverance as a process that involves the past, the present and the future, let's consider 2 Corinthians 1:8, where Paul talks about how they came through some hardship in Asia. He says, "for we would not, brethren, have you ignorant of our troubles which came to us in Asia that we were pressed out of measure, above strength, insomuch that we despaired even of life".

Have you faced such pressure before to the point where you do not even know whether you want to live or die? This was what happened to Paul and his companions. But he says in verse 9, "we had the sentence of death in ourselves so that we should not trust in ourselves, but in God which raises the dead." In other words, in his pressures, difficulties, and fight with the enemy, he found meaning: he was under a sentence of death – death to himself so that he would not trust in himself, but trust in the living God. Just that meaning alone gives him peace.

The implication of this for me, as a believer, is that in the midst of my trouble, whatever the enemy is doing, God is actually doing something within it. If I connect to that, I will be able to relate with whatever is happening around me from the place of strength.

The key message here is that if we are not connecting with what the Lord is doing within us at the moment, we will relate only with what the devil is doing outside against us and that only produces fear and hopelessness, and not faith. If I know my God is busy in me, even with the worst of the devil, whatever the devil is doing outside of me doesn't so affect me as to cause a breakdown. I will have the peace of mind, the presence of mind to stay with God, while He works in my life; and from the place of strength and authority I can then go against the devil.

Verse 10 of the same passage says, "Who delivers us from so great a death, and doth deliver; in whom we trust He will yet deliver us." The full nature of deliverance is portrayed here – He delivered us from so great a death; He doth deliver now; He will yet deliver. This confirms that deliverance is truly in three phases. He delivered us, He is delivering us now, and He will yet deliver us. A very dear wonderful man of God put it this way: "The first level of deliverance is to take us from the devil. You are saved, you are brought into the Kingdom and the devil is kicked out of you. That is the first level." You are out of the devil and the devil is out of you now; but he is still interested in you. You probably have some stuff in your life that he wants to use to destroy you, such as your family background, which brings us to the next level: warfare.

WARFARE

Warfare is important. Warfare is taking authority. Then again, even that can be abused. We should be taking authority in faith, and we should be conscious that our prayer is having impact. And let me say this: the greatest warfare does not consist in binding the devil, but in knowing and fulfilling your purpose.

If you really want to disarm the devil, become knowledgeable about what you are called to do in life, about what your role is, and give attention to that. Once you give attention to your role, you come into meaning, you gain momentum, and your life becomes fruitful. If you do not know your role or you are not consciously fulfilling your role, while busy doing warfare after warfare, you are likely to become frustrated and hopeless. You will say, "I have been binding the devil all my life and I am not seeing changes". Have you found your purpose? Are you fulfilling it? That is what will give you meaning more than anything. It is the best way to wound the devil.

"The greatest level of warfare does not consist in binding the devil, but in knowing and fulfilling your purpose."

But, having said that, warring is important. Paul said, "I have fought a good fight, I have finished my course, I have kept the faith" (2 Timothy 4:7). These are the three things which are crucial. In order to run your race, you must fight the fight, but again your faith is more important than the fight. More importantly, your faith is the victory. It is the reason for the fight. If you are merely fighting because you want to survive, or want to have some extra money, it will be frustrating. But when you have a given purpose for which you are fighting, the fight becomes meaningful because the fight is part of the process and so you will be excited.

You are not scared of the devil. Why? Because now you are fighting for a reason. He is fighting a lost battle but you are fighting for a reason. You are fighting for a dream. You have a purpose to your life.

LIFE OF DOMINION

As you go on warring, learning, becoming more like your Father, it brings you to the third level, which is dominion. You come into your dominion as a child of God. You come into an understanding of your exalted position in Christ. At this point in your journey, the presence of evil becomes meaningless and is no longer a threat to you. So when you are going through the process, there is no need to be confused; there is no need to become hopeless or frustrated; there is no need to begin to think that the devil is so powerful. No, he is not so powerful; he is a creature. God uses him too to fulfill purposes in our lives. Your purpose is far more important than the threat of the devil. As you go through the process, you come to a place of dominion, which positions you to exercise Kingdom authority. Thereafter, you are ready to help others, not just to seek help. Then you are in a position to know that the presence of darkness does not threaten light.

When light is shining, darkness will retreat. The presence of evil is not a threat to good. You are now in dominion. Satan is still an enemy - you still fight him, he still fights you - but he is not a threat to you. David said it this way, "Thou preparest a table before me in the presence of my enemies. Thou anointest my head with oil, my cup runneth over" (Psalms 23:5). The presence of the enemy does not even stop you from enjoying the table of the Lord.

Here is a recap of the things I have said in this chapter. Understanding that there is a process to deliverance will help us to have the right frame of mind when we are going through that process. It will keep us from being confused. A lot of people become confused and frustrated because of a lack of understanding on the process of deliverance. If you meet someone who was oppressed and bound by the devil and you start to kick the demon out of them, the devil is going to fight back. The Bible puts it this way:

> *"When the unclean spirit is gone out of a man, he walketh through dry places, seeking rest, and findeth none. Then he saith, I will return into my house from whence I came out; and when he is come, he findeth it empty, swept, and garnished. Then goeth he, and taketh with himself seven other spirits more wicked than himself, and they enter in and dwell there: and the last state of that man is worse than the first..." (Matthew 12:43-45).*

This means that when demons are in a human life, they regard that life as their home. When you kick them out, giving them an eviction notice and they become homeless, it affects their ability to manifest their evil nature, so they feel pain. Consequently, they will definitely seek to return; and when they do so and find their former abode empty, they solicit the help of seven other spirits even more wicked and this means that when they find their way back into the person, his or her state becomes worse.

This is not a discouragement for deliverance; rather it is an encouragement for proper deliverance. The person being delivered has to be willing to come into the Kingdom of God, to receive Jesus Christ, and be born again. And we, who are ministering the deliverance, must carefully take that person through counseling. There is a time when you just don't want to keep knocking them down, you want to counsel, you want to go into the details and find out what has really gone wrong with the people to whom you are ministering. Then, as part of that counseling process, you take the time to apply the power meaningfully. It takes power to break the curse, to break the yoke. Power breaks the yoke. Then you bring on the Word of God into the life of the person who is being delivered and they must be encouraged to develop a personal love for God's Word. God's Word is God Himself in print. As the person feeds on that Word, the Word cleanses and teaches reverence to God.

At this point I will have to say more about the cleansing aspect, as I said I would earlier. The Book of 2 Corinthians 7:1-2 says, "Having therefore these promises, dearly beloved, let us cleanse ourselves from all filthiness of the flesh and spirit, perfecting holiness in the fear of God." In other words, there are two major aspects of cleansing that need to happen within the process of deliverance – the cleansing of contaminations in the spirit and the cleansing of contaminations of the flesh.

Let me explain it this way. The devil often seizes grounds in the spirit. He is an aggressor. He takes those grounds piece by piece. When we come into the Kingdom, we are restored to God's inheritance; however, it takes a gradual process to recover some things. It is like God bringing the children of Israel from Egypt through the wilderness into the land of Canaan - the land of promise, the land flowing with milk and honey, the good and large land. However, that land had to be taken territory by territory. The ability to take those territories also was predicated on their obedience to God.

This is the process. There is no magic wand. It is the process that works the wonders. People who are seeking deliverance must be people who want to be like God, who want to end up in heaven - not just wanting to have an easier life here without caring about God or heaven. That is not real deliverance.

There is a lot of stuff out there that is not real deliverance. I call it recycled bondage. Real deliverance is cleansing and reclaiming the portions of an individual's life in the spirit realm, as well as dealing with the many physical doorways that were opened for the enemy to invade. Such doorways include doors of sexual sin, witchcraft, demonic inheritance or contaminated dwellings. I will give these details later on - but cleansing is a process, it is a major part of the process, and doesn't happen in just one day.

There are tools that are needed for thorough cleansing. We need the Word of God. And we need the Blood of Jesus because that is the legal ground. The Blood continues to be relevant but the Word does the washing. We also need what the Bible calls the fear of the Lord. He says, perfecting holiness (that is maturing in holiness), in the fear (or out of fear) of God.

We need to know the fear of God. It is not a negative thing. It is one of the most beneficial aspects of our Christian heritage. It is our reverence for God - our personal choice to respect God in our life, conduct, and in the choices we make that will keep us purified in life. The Bible says, "The fear of the Lord is clean, enduring forever…"(Psalm 19:9). The fear of the Lord as an attribute or character will keep us cleansed and purified from contamination with evil.

This is so important when demons are cast out of someone. As I mentioned before, demons will always try to come back. They will try to lure the individual by providing temptations that used to work effectively in the past. Most times, this approach doesn't work for those who have truly received the love of God. They can resist and not yield. But the demons won't give up easily. If you are not yielding to temptations, then they will try to persecute you, to make life difficult for you in other ways - in the hope that, by doing so, they can frustrate you and somehow open a doorway to return.

When this fails, they will try to blackmail and manipulate you through demonically generated dreams. The objective is to confuse you into thinking you are not delivered. Do not panic. Instead, immerse yourself in the atmosphere of worship and meditation in the Word of God. The devil will soon flee from you. Be steadfast and unmovable.

> "Be sober, be vigilant; because your adversary the devil, as a roaring lion, walketh about, seeking whom he may devour: Whom resist stedfast in the faith, knowing that the same afflictions are accomplished in your brethren that are in the world. But the God of all grace, who hath called us unto his eternal glory by Christ Jesus, after that ye have suffered a while, make you perfect, stablish, strengthen, settle you. To him be glory and dominion for ever and ever. Amen" (1 Peter 5:8-11).

Chapter Five

THE GOD WHO DELIVERS

"Moreover he said, I am the God of thy father, the God of Abraham, the God of Isaac, and the God of Jacob. And Moses hid his face; for he was afraid to look upon God. And the LORD said, I have surely seen the affliction of my people which are in Egypt, and have heard their cry by reason of their taskmasters; for I know their sorrows; And I am come down to deliver them out of the hand of the Egyptians, and to bring them up out of that land unto a good land and a large, unto a land flowing with milk and honey; unto the place of the Canaanites, and the Hittites, and the Amorites, and the Perizzites, and the Hivites, and the Jebusites. Now therefore, behold, the cry of the children of Israel is come unto me: and I have also seen the oppression wherewith the Egyptians oppress them. Come now therefore, and I will send thee unto Pharaoh, that thou mayest bring forth my people the children of Israel out of Egypt" (Exodus 3:7-10).

THE COVENANT KEEPING GOD

Deliverance is a deliberate act of a loving God to rescue His people. I want you to see something in the above Bible passage, as revealed by the Almighty God. God, the Father of our Lord Jesus Christ, is the only authentic Savior and Deliverer. His redemptive works on the earth constitute an unfolding revelation of His love, compassion, and commitment to His creation.

Look at those words again: "I have surely seen the affliction of my people which are in Egypt, and have heard their cry by reason of their taskmasters; for I know their sorrows; And I am come down to deliver them out of the hand of the Egyptians..." Wow! He is the God that delivers.

Again, I want you to carefully take note of how He identifies Himself in this passage. He says, "I am the God of thy father, the God of Abraham, the God of Isaac, and the God of Jacob". Why does He identify Himself this way? Because there is a covenant in place. In this particular instance, it is a covenant referring to the children of Israel. It was a direct covenant with Abraham, which He repeated to Isaac and then to Jacob, to bind Himself to the Jewish people or to the descendants of Abraham. They had now been over 400 years in the land of Egypt and according to the terms of this covenant, God had not forgotten. He had come down to deliver them.

I believe that the children of Israel in that generation who were going through those severe trials, difficulties, pains, and oppression had not reckoned with the fact that they had a covenant that was covering them and that, on the basis of that covenant, God would act on their behalf as they cried out. Suddenly, their cry prevailed and God, on the basis of His covenant, came down to deliver them, through the ministry of Prophet Moses.

Here, again, I must emphasize that even though God will use human beings to bring help to other human beings, for that is His chosen method, we have to be careful to remember that God will not share His glory with anybody. It is God who delivers. And He does this because He loves us, His people.

You may be saying, "Well, He was available to deliver the Israelites because He had a covenant with Abraham, Isaac, and Jacob, and so He had to deliver the Jewish people". Of course, we also have a covenant. It is called the Everlasting Covenant – the eternal one – no beginning, no end. And that covenant is found in Jesus Christ, the Son of the Living God. "Behold the lamb of God that taketh away the sins of the world" (John 1:29).

By reason of the sacrifice, the blood sacrifice of Jesus Christ, we have entered - both Jews and Gentiles - into a superior covenant. It is not a covenant based upon the blood of goats, calves, bulls, sheep or any other animal but upon the Blood of His only Begotten Son. As the Bible says, "Neither by the blood of goats and calves, but by his own blood he entered in once into the holy place, having obtained eternal redemption for us" (Hebrews 9:12).

THE EVERLASTING COVENANT

There is this one covenant that is eternal in scope and dimension that, today, men and women can plug into - and whatsoever be the curse or covenant that provided the enemy the avenue for oppression, it can be instantly broken as we exercise faith in the Lord Jesus Christ.

I really want to re-emphasize this because, often, when people are desperate to be free from their shackles, disease, and pain, they tend to focus on their situations to such an extent that would almost promote or elevate their unwanted conditions to the place of a god. Then, desperate to do anything prescribed by both authentic and non-authentic ministers or deliverers who are offering help, they can miss the whole point.

Deliverance comes from a God who cares. We cannot seek deliverance apart from a relationship of commitment to Him. He is committed to us and has made a way so that we can have the desire to know Him. The Bible says

> *"Then said Jesus to those Jews which believed on him, If ye continue in my word, then are ye my disciples indeed; And ye shall know the truth, and the truth shall make you free" (John 8:31-32).*

Progressive encounter with the truth of God's Word can only result from a committed relationship of true discipleship, and this in turn will impart liberty to the various components of our lives that the enemy has seized. The more we encounter God, the more we become free – free to be like Him and free to be whom we are called to be. People seeking deliverance must have a desire for God or must be encouraged to develop an appetite for God.

If people do not want God, they may want to pay for their deliverance. It is important to let them know that it doesn't work that way. Deliverance ministers are not magicians. Deliverance ministers do not act in their own authority. They have no power to act in their own authority. They have a term of reference. They are not allowed to go beyond the Word of God to do anything.

It is good to appreciate and celebrate the men and women who are anointed and called into deliverance ministry to help the multitudes of people; but it is very important as well to know that God is the One who delivers. One of the benefits of this realization is that deliverance will not end with the deliverance minister. Every day in your home, in your dream state, the Holy Spirit is busy enforcing your deliverance. In fact, David said, "Thou wilt keep me from trouble while you encompass me about with songs of deliverance" (Psalm 32:7). It is one thing to be delivered from a situation, but it is yet another to have your deliverance as a living reality because you are carrying God around.

God and bondage do not coexist. So, I encourage you to get rid of your demons, seek to grow in your character to become more and more like God, and seek to love the Lord and follow Him.

"Every day in your home, in your dream state, the Holy Spirit is busy enforcing your deliverance."

Chapter Six

THE ORIGIN, FALL AND CAREER OF THE DEVIL

There is a treasury of information in the Word of God regarding the origin, fall, and the career of the devil. Just to put that into perspective, let us look at some Scriptures. We will start with Ezekiel 28:11-13

> *"Moreover the word of the Lord came unto me, saying, Son of man, take up a lamentation upon the king of Tyrus, and say unto him, Thus saith the Lord God; Thou sealest up the sum, full of wisdom, and perfect in beauty. Thou hast been in Eden the garden of God; every precious stone was thy covering, the sardius, topaz, and the diamond, the beryl, the onyx, and the jasper, the sapphire, the emerald, and the carbuncle, and gold: the workmanship of thy tabrets and of thy pipes was prepared in thee in the day that thou wast created"*

The above description, apparently, couldn't have been for a human being. First, while man was made from the dust; this creature was made of precious stones. Notwithstanding, it is clearly stated that the creature is not self-existing but was created. Moreover, the Bible says that he was perfect in beauty and full of wisdom. In fact, he sealed up the sum. He represented what we could call perfect-perfect.

Not only that, of this creature, it is stated that music was imputed into him—organs, flutes, all kinds of music. What was the reason for God putting music into this very powerful, excellent being? It was because he was created to lead worship in heaven.

Verse 14 of the passage goes further to say:

> *"Thou art the anointed cherub that covereth; and I have set thee so: thou wast upon the holy mountain of God; thou hast walked up and down in the midst of the stones of fire."*

This being was in the very presence of God. He was a cherub, one of the highest levels of angels. He was an anointed cherub that covered the throne of God, a guardian angel. He covered the throne of God with worship, which means he was close to the heart of God. (Don't get disappointed when people who are close to you break your heart. Your Father went through it; you are not the first).

THE FALL

Up until this point, everything about this creature seems incomparable and irreproachable. But we must read further. Verses 15-17: "Thou was perfect in thy ways from the day that thou was created, till iniquity was found in thee…Thine heart was lifted up because of thy beauty, thou hast corrupted thy wisdom by reason of thy brightness: I will cast thee to the ground, I will lay thee before kings, that they may behold thee.

So we have the tragedy of this being and the primary cause laid clearly before us. This powerful being fell. Why? His heart was lifted up because of his beauty. Pride came into his heart because of his beauty. This means that he started looking at himself, instead of looking at God who had made him.

This is where a fall would come from—self-focus and self-centeredness. It comes in all shapes and forms. Not only can you be tempted to keep looking at yourself to see how beautiful you are or how much you have accomplished, but you may also be tempted to focus on yourself, based upon your failures, inadequacies and inabilities. Either way, it is still self-centeredness and can lead to a fall. The scriptural injunction is that we continually look unto Jesus the author and the finisher of our faith (Hebrews 12:2).

So, the first problem of this angel, was that he started to look at his own beauty. Who created him beautiful? God. For who? God beautified him for Himself. But he became filled with pride, rather than giving glory to God. Moreover, the Bible says he corrupted his wisdom by reason of his brightness. Brightness here speaks of insight, intelligence, and inventiveness. This means that this angel was created with wisdom, with which he demonstrated exceptional intelligence. But he soon forgot who gave him the gift of wisdom and began to flatter himself. He thought himself omnipotent and illimitable; forgetting that, being a created being, the One who created him would always be superior to him in every way. And, so, God told him:

"...I will cast thee to the ground, I will lay thee before kings, that they may behold thee. Thou hast defiled thy sanctuaries by the multitude of thine iniquities, by the iniquity of thy traffic; therefore will I bring forth a fire from the midst of thee, it shall devour thee, and I will bring thee to ashes upon the earth in the sight of all them that behold thee" (Verses 17-18).

Note that even though Ezekiel was used to write these lines, the conversation did not happen during his time. The things he recorded were things flowing out of the prophetic womb. I dare to think that he did not understand half of what he was saying but was just bringing forth revelation.

One of the things God said about this being is that he had defiled his sanctuaries by the multitude of his iniquities and by the iniquity of his traffic. This means that not only did he have corrupt ideas, but he actually started pushing them to other angels to corrupt them. As he did, a third of the angels bought into it. That made God to pronounce judgment on him. God declared to him in verse 19: "All they that know thee among the people shall be astonished at thee: thou shalt be a terror, and never shalt thou be any more."

But what exactly is the name of this being? God brings it out clearly in Isaiah 14:12-14:

"How art thou fallen from heaven, O Lucifer, son of the morning! How art thou cut down to the ground, which didst weaken the nations! For thou hast said in thine heart, I will ascend into heaven, I will exalt my throne above the stars of God: I will sit also upon the mount of the

congregation, in the sides of the north: I will ascend above
the heights of the clouds; I will be like the most High."

This being was called Lucifer. And we know that he had a throne, which he said he would exalt above the stars of God. Stars here refer to angels. Now, for Lucifer to say he would ascend to heaven means that he was coming from a place lower than heaven. This provides us with a number of insights. Could it be that, at this point in time, he was a delegate in a rulership capacity? Had God removed him from worship and given him another assignment, and could it be that it was there he began to scheme, saying, "I am not done with my career; I will ascend into heaven, I will exalt my throne above the angels, I will sit on the side of the north"?

The "north" is God's governmental seat. Lucifer's ambition was to take God's place. Not only had he defiled a third of the angels of heaven with his evil ambition but was actually thinking he could unseat the Almighty God. God's reaction to this is contained in verses 15–17:

"Yet thou shalt be brought down to hell, to the sides of the
pit. They that see thee shall narrowly look upon thee, and
consider thee, saying, is this man that made the earth to
tremble, that did shake kingdoms; that made the world as
a wilderness, and destroyed the cities thereof; that opened
not the house of his prisoners?"

God promised him a solid, resounding and permanent defeat.

REBELLION AND DESTRUCTION

I believe Genesis 1 contains some revelations as to the scope and impact of Lucifer's ambition on God's creation. Genesis 1:1 says,

"In the beginning, God created the heavens and the earth." "In the beginning" here refers to the eternal past. However, verse two speaks of chaos and I believe that the rebellion of Lucifer occurred here.

In the Isaiah passage that we read earlier, he boasts, "I will ascend to heaven, I will exalt my throne above the stars, I will sit on the side of the north, and I will be like the Most High." He was already a defiled angel, pushing his idea. We know that God is patient, so none can really tell how many millions of years Lucifer had been faithfully serving God or when exactly he started nursing his ambition. Still, verse 2 tells us, "And the earth was without form, and void; and darkness was upon the face of the deep. And the Spirit of God moved upon the face of the waters."

As I mentioned before, it is generally agreed by most sound Bible scholars that between verses one and two of Genesis chapter one was when Satan's rebellion took place; and at some point in time there was angelic warfare which destroyed the elements of creation. God, then, withdrew light and everything froze. More on this subject can be read from Pastor Benny Hinn's book on "Demons and Angels".

In Genesis 1:3, God said, "Let there be light" and there was light. As you would find in the succeeding verses, this light was not light from the sun or the moon. In fact, the light does not refer to light as we know it. The light here means that the rebellion instigated by Lucifer had passed and God was restoring things again. In essence, God brought back light, where there had been darkness.

Some theologians postulate that the earth is about 6,000 years old but that cannot be correct, unless they are talking about the restored earth. The original creation dates to millions of years. Also when scientists talk about how the earth was formed from a "Big Bang," I believe that they are talking about the angelic warfare that occurred at the time of Lucifer's rebellion. But they do not know what it is, and besides the devil lies to them because he does not want them to know the truth about his first defeat.

"And there was war in heaven: Michael and his angels fought against the dragon; and the dragon fought and his angels, And prevailed not; neither was their place found any more in heaven. And the great dragon was cast out, that old serpent, called the Devil, and Satan, which deceiveth the whole world: he was cast out into the earth, and his angels were cast out with him" (Revelation 12:7-8).

We have so far obtained substantial revelations from these passages about Lucifer, the devil or Satan. We know that he was not created with evil; he was created a beautiful angel. His name was Lucifer, the son of the morning. God invested so much in him but he disappointed God because he started looking at himself. You may be wondering, couldn't God have anticipated that Lucifer would do this? He is Almighty. He is all-knowing, so He would know; yet He did not prevent it; He chose not to.

Does that make God responsible for the rebellion of Lucifer? No - just like you and I cannot claim that the devil is responsible for our actions, even though he tempts us. God never wants us to be automated, motorized dummies that He programs to do stuff without a will of our own. He gives us the free will to love Him or choose not to. Lucifer decided to love himself. Self-love, by the way, is still the basis of all destructions today. It is the major reason why many relationships do not work. People love themselves so much they become inconsiderate of others.

So, in summary, Lucifer loved himself and got flattered by his beauty, wisdom and insight – which were all given to him by God. He thought he could do anything; so he went ahead to push those ideas on others, corrupted himself and rebelled against God. Eventually, this one-time most beautiful, most powerful creature of God became transformed into a hideous enemy. His final place, of course, is the lake of fire.

THE CAREER OF THE DEVIL

In John 10:10, Jesus says,

> *"The thief cometh not, but for to steal, and to kill, and to destroy: I am come that they might have life, and that they might have it more abundantly."*

First and foremost, I want you to see that Lucifer had crafted an opposite kingdom for himself called the kingdom of darkness. This kingdom has an order, a hierarchy, and a governmental structure.

Apostle Paul tells us, by divine inspiration, in Ephesians 6:10-12:

> *"Finally, my brethren, be strong in the Lord, and in the power of his might. Put on the whole armor of God that ye may be able to stand against the wiles of the devil. For we wrestle not against flesh and blood, but against principalities, against powers, against the rulers of the darkness of this world, against spiritual wickedness in high places."*

Principalities rule over territories. Powers are high-ranking former archangels in the service of God who bought into the lie of Lucifer and so fell with him. They willingly serve his doomed purposes today. Rulers of darkness are a level of angelic order that controls the secret things behind the scene. They manipulate and control governance, commerce, religion, finance and the sex industry from behind the scene.

The Bible speaks of a host of wicked spirits in high places causing violence in the earth, doing damage upon the earth. We are ranged against them for mortal combat. There are millions, perhaps billions, of fallen angelic beings and demonic powers. Demons are of lower ranks but they serve the purpose of Lucifer. There are angelic authorities at various levels under the command of Lucifer. They all do his will. They are all enemies of God and enemies of man.

THE CAREER OF THE DEVIL TODAY

The various hierarchies of satanic angels and messengers constitute the kingdom of darkness. Their sole purpose is to hinder the plan of God. Lucifer goes up and down supervising them. We see this in Job 1:6-7:

> *"Now there was a day when the sons of God came to present themselves before the Lord, and Satan came also among them. And the Lord said unto Satan, Whence comest thou? Then Satan answered the Lord, and said, from going to and fro in the earth, and from walking up and down in it."*

The sons of God came to present themselves and Satan came among them. He was not meant to be there. When God asked him where he was coming from, he responded that he was going to and fro the earth, walking up and down it. He has a ministry of walking up and down, going to and from all over the earth. Doing what? He is supervising his own evil works and giving oversight to the assignments he has given to his fellow fallen angels and demons. They have partitioned the earth and the planetary system amongst themselves in order to effectively carry out evil plans upon mankind in the earthly realm; to oppose the things of God; and to attempt to hinder the work of God. This is the focus of their assignment.

Satanic forces control the politics of nations from behind the scene. They control the financial industry, the entertainment industry, sex industry, and they also control violent crimes, murders and wars from behind the scene. They control drug abuse, misuse and trafficking from behind the scene. They control commerce and industry from behind and even control the religious systems of every nation.

Satan's purpose is to seize upon the inheritance of God on the earth that was originally pledged to Adam in Genesis 1, when God created man. Man was created to take over the earth. God created man from a lower material (dust) and breathed upon him the breath of life (divine essence). He put him in charge and gave him governmental authority. He blessed man and charged man to multiply, replenish the earth and fill the earth with their kind. He gave man dominion to have control of the birds of the air and other living beings. He gave man control and authority over the planetary system. Man had control over every beast and creeping thing upon the earth. He had control over the fishes and every creature that passes through the path of the sea.

God was very strategic in giving man authority and control over these three realms. If the devil and his angels are going to function, they will do so from these realm, so God gave man control. God Himself is in charge of the heavens of heavens, but He gave man control of the earth.

If man were to grow into his inheritance, and exercise governmental power, where would Satan be? Satan had only one option, hell. So Satan had to devise a plan, a smart move to seize the inheritance of man and possibly to seize that man and bring him to his side. That was where the temptation happened in the Garden of Eden, and man totally failed, disconnected himself from God and put himself at the disposal of the enemy. But God had a plan of redemption in place.

Satan is reacting to what he can see. He believes himself to be smart, that he has it together and knows how to defeat God; so he reacts to what he can see. But what about the hidden things in the heart of God? That, he cannot see. On the apparent level, he thought he could bring that man to his side, and so he went after Adam and Eve, presenting his manifesto. God stayed aside and allowed man to fail. Once man had disappointed and failed God, He withdrew that God-kind of life and man became a dead spirit inside a body that would die within a thousand years.

Satan began to jubilate with his angels. But God did something to protect man from eternal doom – he sealed off the tree of life. Man would die, but his spirit had to go somewhere. The first man that was given dominion over the earth is just the copy of the real man that was to come. He was not the full potential man. That was just a picture of the real man. The real man was to come thousands of years later. The Bible calls Him the Son of Man and also the Son of God, who is the quickening Spirit, the life-giving Spirit.

You have to understand this to be able to function even in your status as a new creation man. What God did is that, in Adam, He gave man a human body and authority over the earth, born of the flesh; but in Christ He gave man a spirit body, giving him authority in the realm of the spirit. This is the real complete man that God is creating, and that complete man is a terror to the devil with dual citizenship — both earthly and heavenly citizenship in the Spirit realm.

Satan has strategically and politically partitioned the earth and the planetary system among his angels and demons for the purpose of rulership. Remember his original desire: he wants to rule and be worshipped. He is still seeking that today. He is stealing the worship of people by offering them flattering positions and lying to them. They bow down to him; and he gives them influence, and they then go ahead to influence other people. He works within the hierarchy of evil powers. Take religion, for instance; he is far more successful in religion than other areas.

What is the ultimate goal in the career of the devil? Why is he going up and down over the earth? Why does he partition the earth among his demonic hierarchies? What is his ultimate purpose? "The thief cometh not, but for to steal, and to kill, and to destroy" (John 10:10). This is the career of the devil — to steal. To steal from man and cheat him out of his original inheritance. The earth belongs to man. The silver, the gold, everything here belongs to man. The great grandfather of men sold out; so Satan stole what belongs to man and is still using that today to destroy man. He is offering man perverted versions of the original blessings that God gave to him. To destroy means to render people incapable of their original purpose.

What is the original purpose? "Let us make man in our own image, after our likeness, and let them have dominion" (Genesis 1:26). Identity and rulership was God's original purpose for man. Now Satan is corrupting and perverting man. Jesus came to give His life in order to give us two basic things – abundance of grace and the gift of righteousness (Romans 5:17). With these two things we will be able to reign and dominate in life. That was God's original purpose for man. He made man in the image and likeness of Himself and gave him dominion. You need the image of God, and you need your identity in Christ to be in dominion.

What is the purpose of the enemy? To steal man's inheritance and to destroy him, render him incapable of functioning in God's original design and ultimately kill him. "To kill" is not just to attack the body but to separate man permanently from God so that he enters eternal death.

Anything the devil is pushing or promoting is what originally belonged to man. Satan has perverted these things and pushes them on to man so that man is lured away from pursuing his original destiny, his original identity, and by living on those perverted versions of the original, his soul and his potential are destroyed and ultimately he enters into eternal doom. Satan is busy at it. That is why there is capitalism, communism, and all "isms". That is why there is religion of every type. He works through them to destroy man.

It is very difficult these days to separate between what is religion and what is Christianity. Christianity was not intended by God to be a religion. Christianity is divinity coming to man so that man can take his original place of inheritance and rulership.

THE RESTORATION PLANS OF GOD AND THE DEFEAT OF THE DEVIL

The Holy Spirit is upon the earth today to restore man back to his original glory, back to the original intention of God. Jesus came to restore man by giving man a dual citizenship – legal on the earth and legal in the heavens. Jesus says, "I am the door: by me if any man enter in, he shall be saved, and shall go in and out, and find pasture" (John 10:9). Door to what? You might ask. It is the door to the supernatural nature and power of God – Divinity. He said when we enter in through Him, we shall be saved.

The word 'saved' encompasses deliverance from sin, power of sin, and future fear of punishment for sin. It encompasses provision, protection, and preservation. However, after being saved, He says you shall go in and out, and find pasture. This speaks of spiritual adventure. He is simply saying, "Do not be lazy. Do not stick to the flesh. Go in and out of the spirit realm and do business or ministry with what you are anointed with, the gift you have been given." When you do what God has called you to do, you will continue to increase and not diminish in the mighty name of Jesus Christ.

The mandate of the church's five-fold leadership today is to bring out mature manhood in the church, a new creation, properly credentialed on the earth and in the heavens. We are not dealing with mere men, we are dealing with wicked powers that have distributed themselves illegally and are dictating to the earth. We are to dictate to them and unseat them from territories, from families, from governments, from nations, and minister the healing power of God all over the earth.

Picture a militant church robed in the power and glory of God, moving forth in great authority, that have Satan firmly under their feet, who are lovers of and worshippers of God, who carry authority, fulfilling the original mandate of "Let us make man in our image after our likeness and let them have dominion over the beasts and the creeping things of the earth, and over the fishes and whatsoever passes through the path of the sea" (Genesis 1:26).

This is the original mandate that Jesus came to fulfill. That is why He gave His life and that job will be done. There are two opposing kingdoms that are fighting. Jesus said, I will build my church and the gates of hell shall not prevail against it (Matthew 16:18).

When Jesus carried out His ministry, His objective was to reveal to people that there were two kingdoms at war.

"Then was brought unto him one possessed with a devil, blind, and dumb: and he healed him, insomuch that the blind and dumb both spake and saw. And all the people were amazed, and said, Is not this the son of David? But when the Pharisees heard it, they said, This fellow doth not cast out devils, but by Beelzebub the prince of the devils. And Jesus knew their thoughts, and said unto them, Every kingdom divided against itself is brought to desolation; and every city or house divided against itself shall not stand: And if Satan cast out Satan, he is divided against himself; how shall then his kingdom stand? And if I by Beelzebub cast out devils, by whom do your children cast them out? Therefore they shall be your judges. But if I cast out devils by the Spirit of God, then the kingdom of God is come unto you. Or else how can one enter into a strong man's house, and spoil his goods, except he first bind the strong man? and then he will spoil his house. He that is not with me is

against me; and he that gathereth not with me scattereth abroad" (Matthew 12:22-30).

What are we to infer from this? Satan is organized into kingdoms. There are rulers over nations, over cities, over families. There are satanic agents with lieutenants, enforcing the will of the devil. But you are the new sheriff in town and you have come to take over. You are the new sheriff in town! In your family, you are the one who changes the game, and God will help us all to consecrate and pay the price.

Satan has a kingdom – the opposing kingdom, the kingdom of darkness. What Jesus is saying is that He (Jesus) is the Stronger Man. Before Jesus came, there had been a strongman called Satan who was ruling over the earth. Now a Stronger Man has come and has bound him and spoilt his goods. Now He is taking Satan's spoils. That is what the people saw in the form of blind eyes seeing, the lame walking, the dumb speaking – all of these were a sign that the strongman that was in town has been reduced, fired, and a new sheriff has come to town, and His name is Jesus Christ, the Son of the Living God.

"Forasmuch then as the children are partakers of flesh and blood, he also himself likewise took part of the same; that through death he might destroy him that had the power of death, that is, the devil; And deliver them who through fear of death were all their lifetime subject to bondage" (Hebrews 2:14-15).

Because men are flesh and blood and Satan is spirit and he uses that to take advantage of them, Jesus came to do something. He covered Himself with flesh to enable Him to pass through the gates of death. By covering himself with flesh He was able to pass through the gates of death because God cannot die but flesh can die. Satan was the king of death because he was the first to be dead, cut off from the Source of Life. Jesus moved in to withdraw that authority from Satan. By dying, He moved into the realm of the dead, became a member of the dead that He might destroy him and deliver man, and become the King of the dead. When the Father raised Him from the dead, Christ became the First Begotten of the dead, the first to have life from the dead. Satan is still in the dead. He has no divine life. That is only available through Jesus Christ the Son of the living God.

He that hath the Son hath life; and he that hath not the Son of God hath not life 1John 5:12

THE RESSURECTED GLORIOUS SON OF GOD IS OUR PATTERN

John saw Jesus after He was resurrected and he was shaken.

"I was in the Spirit on the Lord's day, and heard behind me a great voice, as of a trumpet, Saying, I am Alpha and Omega, the first and the last:… And when I saw him, I fell at his feet as dead. And he laid his right hand upon me, saying unto me, Fear not; I am the first and the last: I am he that liveth, and was dead; and, behold, I am alive for evermore, Amen; and have the keys of hell and of death." (Revelation 1:11-12; 17-18).

This is how Christ took the key from Satan. Jesus said, "I am the Almighty God. I was dead, and now I am alive forevermore and have the keys of hell and death. Satan no longer has them." The "keys of hell and death" means the authority over hell and death.

Satan used to have the authority of hell and death but no longer has them. Jesus has them. Jesus defeated him and has given you and me the authority of His name.

> *"Let this mind be in you, which was also in Christ Jesus: Who, being in the form of God, thought it not robbery to be equal with God: But made himself of no reputation, and took upon him the form of a servant, and was made in the likeness of men: And being found in fashion as a man, he humbled himself, and became obedient unto death, even the death of the cross. Wherefore God also hath highly exalted him, and given him a name which is above every name: That at the name of Jesus every knee should bow, of things in heaven, and things in earth, and things under the earth; And that every tongue should confess that Jesus Christ is Lord, to the glory of God the Father" (Philippians 2:5-11).*

Do you see all of this? Jesus is Lord in heaven; He is Lord on earth; He is Lord under the earth. So, where is Satan lord? No place! That is why he is illegal everywhere. Anywhere Satan asserts authority, he is illegal. You are here as a delegate of Jesus Christ to remind Satan of this reality and to enforce the law of God on him.

Jesus has given you dual citizenship – citizenship of the earth from being born by your father and mother, which is the only legal way to gain citizenship on the earth; as well as citizenship in the heavens by being born again of the Spirit of God, which is the only legal way to assert authority in the heavens. You have both, so you are Satan's worst nightmare - but he tries to devalue you by making you to think you are less than what you are. When we lose our sense of identity, he can cause us to play his game of defeat and condemnation.

Living in the presence of God is vital, otherwise you would be fighting from below up, which is frustrating. But when you live in His presence, you dictate downwards; so always seek His presence. It is the only way to go.

> *"And you, being dead in your sins and the uncircumcision of your flesh, hath he quickened together with him, having forgiven you all trespasses; Blotting out the handwriting of ordinances that was against us, which was contrary to us, and took it out of the way, nailing it to his cross; And having spoiled principalities and powers, he made a shew of them openly, triumphing over them in it"*
> *(Colossians 2:13-15).*

Yes, we were dead in our sins through our uncircumcised flesh. We were responding to the passions and promptings of the devil. Now, Christ has given us supernatural life together with Him to get out of the grave of this death and corruption called this world. In Christ Jesus, God defeated the devil and made a parade of him before all his hosts of angels. They witnessed Jesus stripping the devil of all authority, taking away the keys of hell and death from him, and him shaking like a leaf. So any time you and I come in the name of Jesus, Satan has no option.

There are three levels of death: the first is spiritual death. You and I were in the realm of the first level of death. As soon as we are born into this world, we are dead on arrival spiritually. The second level is physical death. If you go through the second level without having spiritual life, you enter into the third level of death, eternal death. Satan abides in eternal death. Jesus entered eternal death for us and came back out. That's why He said,

"For thou wilt not leave my soul in hell; neither wilt thou suffer thine Holy One to see corruption." (Psalm 16:10).

You and I must know we have authority. Declare: "I have authority and every devil is subject to me through the name of the Lord Jesus Christ!"

Chapter Seven

SOME SIGNS OF DEMONIC OPPRESSION

Watch out carefully for these signs, as they are, more often than not, telltale indications of demonic oppression or influence.

1. Exaggerated patterns of human behavior

When an individual exhibits excessive, obsessive, and compulsive traits, there is usually an underlying demonic current fueling such behaviors. An overwhelming sense of helplessness in certain aspects of a person's character may be as a result binding demonic influence.

2. Addiction to chemical substances

The repeated use of alcohol and psychotropic substances will attract demonic spirits to move in and create scars and altars in the human soul, whereby the human will-power is eroded, the emotions disrupted, and a crippling sense of helplessness is generated. Most addictions will fit into this pattern.

3. Mysterious illnesses

Certain types of sickness that defy medical diagnosis may simply be manifestation of demonic oppression. Sometimes people feel certain symptoms but the conditions cannot be detected by x-rays, ultrasound or CAT scan. This is usually because the demons precipitating the conditions can hide away from x-ray pictures and so forth. This can also be true in certain types of missed diagnoses. The missed diagnosis is simply as a result of demonic manipulations to complicate the process and further the affliction.

In 2007, towards the end of a forty-day fasting and prayer period in my life, my younger daughter came down with a severe pain and for a couple of days was really sick. I hesitated to rush into prayer over her, so my wife advised to take her to the hospital. The CAT scan revealed ovarian cyst and she was barely thirteen years at the time. I monitored things closely and concluded it was demonic so I refused to panic. On the last day of my fast, we were in a church service, deep in worship, when I suddenly felt nudged by the Lord to call for those needing deliverance and healing. My daughter stepped forward and the glory of God fell upon her and the demon of ovarian cyst and all the symptoms vanished forever. Hallelujah! Blessed be the name of the Lord forevermore.

4. Across-the-board horizontal family reverses

You might notice similar pattern of struggle in the life of all or most family members. Some families tend to experience the pain of untimely death among family members. This could be due to hidden covenants and curses which need to be located and neutralized. For other families, it might be repeat patterns of failed or late marriages. Yet others might be dealing with cycles of debilitating generational sicknesses where mother or father dealt with it and now the children are also dealing with it.

5. Living below potentials

In John 11, the Lord Jesus raised Lazarus from the dead but he emerged from the tomb having his hands and feet bound. Jesus said to others who could further help him to lose him and let him go. There are wonderful individuals with great potential but demonic shackles and constraints effectively limit or altogether neutralize their ability to actualize dreams or goals.

6. Unexplainable delays

This occurs when nearly everything you do is a victim of unreasonable delays. We all can sometimes experience uncomfortable delays in life and such seasons can prove to be times of great learning or growth in character; but other times even the simplest of tasks like just processing a passport seems to take on a life of its own in protracted delay. When this pattern of delays is common in almost anything you do in life, it may be indicative of the presence of a resisting evil power. Witchcraft spirits and ancestral powers specialize in delay and abort tactics.

7. Failure at the edge of success

This is another form of a delay tactic of the enemy but it is mostly administered by the delegated ancestral power of the family. It is a high ranking power and unlike the other scavenger spirits, this one mainly targets the appointed season of lifting or promotions in the life of the saints. This spirit, if not detected early and neutralized, can deliver punishing blows by repeatedly aborting your appointed seasons which can lead to barrenness in life.

8. Unidentified moving objects

Feeling of crawling and unseen moving objects through parts of the body may indicate demonic presence. In extreme cases, people report somebody pulling their hair and this can sometimes lead to actual depletion of the hair. Sometimes the feeling of movements can be both external and internal. Simply put, unidentified moving objects in the body are demon spirits.

9. Mood swings

Exaggerated or extreme mood swings - from being happy one moment to being depressed and even suicidal the next – is a sign that must not be ignored. Internal emotional disturbances, torments, turmoil, self-hate and in some cases cutting; extreme or overriding feelings of anger, revenge, murder, loneliness, isolation, fear, guilt, and rejection indicate demonic undercurrents.

10. Unbridled religiosity

Sense of religious superiority (holier-than-thou attitude), exalting visions and revelations above the written Word of God, critical and religious gossips, fear of man rather than fear of God (group loyalty including over-veneration of the ministers of God), denominationalism (putting your church above the Body of Christ), doctrines of demons, tolerance of immorality while claiming spirituality (spirit of lawlessness or iniquity) all indicate troubled waters of demonic activity.

11. Haunted homes and cursed items

When you move into certain homes, business places or bring cursed items into your home, the home and the surrounding environment are immediately greeted with oppression. In some cases, this could result in sudden reverse in fortunes. Poltergeist activities might commence, whereby things move around and noises are heard without human involvement. Other times, people might move into a new home and be greeted with unexplainable quarrels among family members and general lack of peace. This is normally the effect of witchcraft or voodoo involvements by previous occupants of the home or business.

12. Hearing voices, seeing or being followed by people visible to you and not others

This can be a fairly difficult situation, requiring warfare prayer, intercession, and judgment of a mature counselor to successfully handle. I find that in most cases of this nature, there is usually a background of what I call inherent or latent occult abilities. This can be as a result of mediumistic activity whereby somebody in the ancestral line was a medium and so remnant of residual occult ability continues down the line but potentially latent in the succeeding generations. When people from this type of background come to Christ and start to participate in spiritual exercises like fasting and spiritual warfare, the latent ability is triggered, and confusion and a state of semi-psychosis is generated. The veil between the physical and spiritual is illegally activated and the occult demon unleashes confusing conditions that can be potentially lethal to the mental stability of the victim. Like I said, cases like this require real skill, insight, judgment of mature counsel, and medical support may be enlisted alongside deliverance ministry. The victim must be counseled to focus on the written Word of God as the basis for immediate and ongoing reality. This requires real skill.

13. The dream state

The dream state is a spiritual gateway into the spirit realm. Once your body is rested and asleep, your spirit functions and interacts with what you are in touch with. There are three types of dreams that can come to you: (1) Dreams that come from God – called divine revelations; (2) Dreams that come from yourself – manifestations of your state; and (3) Dreams that come from the devil – manipulations. The last two can reveal valuable information about conditions requiring deliverance in your life. Some examples include being pursued and shot at; sexual activities with persons known and unknown including, sometimes with animals/creatures; eating food (meal offerings); and waking up to find spiritual exercises a drag. I must here emphasize that all dreams do not necessarily indicate demonic activity; we must rely on The Holy Spirit who will give us necessary insight.

However, there can be an even deeper reality in spiritual state that manifests in dreams. These can be indicative of an area of need. Particularly, this can happen in seasons of consecration when you are seeking God or seeking to be closer with God and something just shows up in your dream characteristically that throws confusion in your mind. By dreaming of wearing your teenage school uniform or your elementary school uniform, going to school like you use to go some thirty to forty years ago, and in the dream you have no consciousness of your adulthood, you are just blending in, something is wrong there. Some have dreams of oppression, whereby someone known or unknown comes and has sexual intercourse with them with all the associated feelings, something is wrong there. Some have dreams of being naked; it is indicative of an area of trouble where you need help.

Chapter Eight

DEMONIC DOORWAYS

"He that diggeth a pit shall fall into it; and whoso breaketh an hedge, a serpent shall bite him" (Ecclesiastes 10:8)

There are no limits to our lives but there are boundaries that have been clearly set by God. Boundaries exist to protect us. If you look at the Levitical priesthood, there were so many restrictions. Most of these are not necessary for salvation today, but they are very helpful in living a good life, whether it is in the area of dieting, in the area of social relationships, or our economic and financial lives. That is why, if you look at the days of Jesus, anytime anyone felt threatened with being thrown out of the synagogue, they were very careful because everything was regulated around the spiritual. If someone was cast out of the synagogue in those days, it was as if their entire life was taken from them; so they were always very careful.

That said, the important point is that there are boundaries. Under the Levitical law, a father must not see his daughter's nakedness. One must not uncover his father's nakedness, or his mother-in-law's, etc. There are moral codes that are meant to keep us from demonic openings. Satan will seek to open grounds in our lives in order for him to come in. He cannot readily jump on you, or anybody else for that matter. The door somehow, somewhere, must be open to him and then he will work. That is why the Bible says "He that diggeth a pit…" (Ecclesiastes 10:8). Digging a pit is a way of creating avenues for the enemy. It further says that if you break a wall – a wall is for protection – then the serpent will bite.

Let us identify some doorways through which demons find entrance:

"Idolatry is a huge doorway that has generational curses."

1. Through the religious activities of your parents

Whatever your parents were into religion-wise has generational values. God was very particular in His restrictions. He said no worshipping of things that were made whether in heaven, in the earth, or beneath the earth or any likeness of anything. Why? Idolatry is a huge doorway that has generational curses.

This is one big problem with many of us from Africa and also other areas of the world. Our parents were not always believers in Jesus Christ; and others, even when they practiced some form of Christianity, did not practice it the correct way. When we talk about religion, we mean all forms of religion, whether Islam, Buddhism, Shintoism, and even some pseudo-Christian professions that are not based on Bible standards for salvation.

2. From the womb

How can a child who is not even born, who is still in the womb, be demonically exposed? It is through the involvement of the parents. Whatever the parent does exposes the child. I know, for instance, that from my own experience, my mother was a very ardent participant of a marine religion. She served marine spirits, had relationships with marine spirits, and used marine power to protect her children and to fight for the fortunes of her children. Even when my elder brother became fantastically rich in those days and I gave my life to the Lord and began to fight against the marine spirit, she told me that she was from marine, and everything that we had come from that source. It was for this reason, among others, that I was rebellious against the family's wealth as it produced a lot of ungodliness.

Right through my deliverance, and even after my deliverance, one of the battles I fought in my life was with the marine spirit because of the way it functions. If a mother has it in her life while giving birth to her children, that demon spirit continues to regard the children as its own children. So you might be seeing your mother in dreams but it may not be your mother, it might be the marine spirit. Even during my deliverance, it was the most difficult area on which to gain a handle. I would literally see myself wandering all over in my dreams with my mom hand in hand, walking and talking. I would wake up and know that it was not my mother – it was the marine spirit.

At last, I finally just cried unto God and said "can you just help me so that when I am in my dream moving about with this spirit, I will know it is not my mother." Then, one day, we were hand in hand moving all over the place I just heard what seemed like a phone call inside me. "You are in a dream state and you are with the marine spirit. This is not your mother." I looked at it, she had that mischievous smile. I said, "You are not my mother, you are marine. The Blood of Jesus! The Blood of Jesus!" She vanished.

Another day, I was in the same dream state again, I recognized her again, and I said, "You are not my mother." My mother was semi-literate and could not speak the Queen's English, but this spirit would speak fluent English. So I knew. I started to plead the Blood, and she said, "It will not work for you this time around." I plead the Blood, and nothing happened. I said, "Lord, what is happening?" He said, "Because you are living in unforgiveness and malice with your roommate, you cannot be claim the promise of God and violate the Word". That is why I say to people that my battles with the devil taught me godliness and in a lot of ways taught me the Word of God. That is why deliverance for me is not just theory or book matter – it is something very real. I learnt some things by Satan's constant attack of me.

I have also seen pregnant women taking their pregnancies to the coven. On the flip side, I have also seen women who are born again, filled with the Holy Ghost, whose babies in the womb would fight with them in warfare, because such babies are spirit beings. Remember that John the Baptist was filled with the Holy Ghost in his mother's womb. Children are spirits. So, depending on what the parent is in touch with or receiving help from, the child can become exposed while in the womb.

3. Parental disobedience to God has implications on children

You will readily remember Achan in the Book of Joshua. God instructed His people that they should not touch any of the spoils of Jericho. But Achan lusted after a Babylonian garment and a wedge of gold and brought defeat to Israel's camp. When judgment was to fall for that sin, it did not only affect him but his wife and children also. So as parents, we carry a heavy responsibility.

The thing you do as a father has impact over four generations. The choices you make as a father will continue to have impact. I think if we really know the implications of these things, we would not be anxious about bringing children into the world. Really, when you are younger you are so excited about having children, especially if you are African. Children are awesome, but there is a huge spiritual responsibility that comes with them.

What did Jesus say concerning Judas? He said, "The Son of man goeth as it is written of him: but woe unto that man by whom the Son of man is betrayed! it had been good for that man if he had not been born" (Matthew 26:24). So, while it is good to have children, we must always be mindful that it is such a responsibility spiritually. This awareness will shake us up a little bit. Training and upbringing of children must be taken seriously.

4. Occult involvement

Any form of occult involvement, whether inherent occult ability, or formal occult enlistment, is a demonic doorway. What do I mean by inherent occult ability? If your grandparents were involved in the occult, first and foremost, you are a member. When people get involved in the occult, they do not only swear their own allegiance, they hand over their children and their children's children as well. Your parents involvement means you are already a member, even without any willingness or contribution on your part. That is why you sometimes marvel when you see yourself in certain dream situations - you have become implicated in things you never formally engage in.

But there are other formal occult involvements, where you can enlist as a member and start receiving materials and instructions; in fact, some will contact you. Since my wife and I have been in the United States, we have been contacted. We once received a letter saying, "We are sorry to say that we have investigated you, and have seen your spiritual potential and with your agreement by signing this letter, we are sending this material to you free of cost." The senders even went as far as to tell us how expensive the material was and to furnish us with a list of names of people who had been members all the way from presidents down. I replied one to say, "the Blood of Jesus!" and seized the opportunity to reply with the gospel message. For others, I just ripped up their letters.

So, the occult certainly does contact people. Now when you get involved and start reading their materials and patronizing them, that is a doorway. Satan is a spiritual prostitute who wants to pollute all and sundry. There are some occult involvements that don't seem so serious but they create some form of a soul tie. For instance, I was in a coffee shop to get coffee. While there, I saw so many wonderful Hispanic people, all lined up, carrying their cups. I imagined they were going on a trip. But I later discovered that there was a man there, a medium, with a spirit of snake, and they were all lined up to receive divination from him. By doing that, they were exposing themselves and their children's children.

Have you seen people reading the stars? Or those preparing or consulting horoscope which they claim can make predictions about your life? Don't be deceived - stargazing or star-reading is basically exposing yourself to witchcraft. It is a very dangerous practice to be reading stars. Once you do that, you are exposing your destiny to demonic investigations which you think is just about receiving information and nothing is done to you. They will modulate, reprogram and steal your destiny. Star-reading is a medium of exposure to demonic infiltration.

5. Demonic Material possession

A lot of the time we travel to different cultures and acquire pieces of art work. In December 1994, I attended a function in Thailand. Besides the business side, there was a tourism side to my trip, and Thailand makes big revenue from tourism. Some of the ladies that were in the same hotel as us went out and visited Buddha temples in the name of sight-seeing. One of the ladies during the visit tied a red ribbon to her wrist. What do you think that was? That was occult initiation straight away! They were not aware, but it had entered their lives and would have consequences and problems until maybe when that person gives her life to Jesus Christ.

6. Demonic transference from other people

Demons can transfer from one person to the other by close association. A more common type is by lovers who are not covered – intimate relationships that are not covered.

I remember the story of this wonderful woman who used to love the Lord and was very dedicated to His service for some fifteen years as a single woman. Later, for some reasons, she left her church and severed her relationship with her pastor. A report came back later that this wonderful sister had started dating and sleeping with a man who was a high priest of the devil, whom she said she hoped to convert. Unknown to her, immediately she started sleeping with that man, the exchange of body fluid is an offering on the devil's altar already. Demons are immediately transferred.

However, it doesn't even have to be an association as deep as this for demons to be transferred. That is why in church, you really have to be aware. I talk a lot about my wife. She is popular anywhere I go. I remember when I was in Atlanta and she was in Africa, there was this lady who told me that when my wife returned, she wanted her to be her prayer partner. I thought that was wonderful. I was anxious to tell my wife because that was one of my friends. I told my wife and she said, "I will pray about it." I was really mad with her because the lady was really reaching out to her. But my wife kept saying she would pray about it. However, shortly before we left Atlanta, my eyes were opened to the fact that this "woman of God" was very deadly spiritually. Can you imagine someone like that becoming your prayer partner – killing you whilst praying with you?

Church is meant to be about fellowship, not mere relationship. When you and I are close, it is a type of fellowship. Fellowship means sharing. Sharing means I am taking a part of you and you are taking a part of me. The person you are close to, sometimes even while you are reading a book, you can hear their voice if you are sensitive in the spirit. If they have been giving you spiritual advice, helping you, you will see them in your dreams sometimes when the Lord wants to talk to you. It is because you are sharing. That is why the Bible says if any believer is a fornicator, a railer, or an extortioner, do not eat with them. It says have nothing to do with them. If someone who is not a believer is fornicating, you can define your relationship level; but the one who is a believer, who is practicing these things and you are yoked together with them, a transfer takes place.

In other words, when you are close to people, let your light shine out, and let their light shine out and there will be fellowship. If it is not light to light, demonic transfer can occur. This especially concerns your close friends. Watch out for gossip. Do not allow gossip between you and another Christian. That is spiritual carelessness. Let the basis of your relationship with your brothers and your sisters be the Lord Himself.

There are people who like to exchange clothing items. This can pose a risk of demonic intrusion. When you wear someone's clothes, there is a spiritual transfer. Look at it from a positive light too. Sometimes God wants me to impart my anointing, especially on the field, when I am under the power of God, and the Holy Spirit would lead me to put my cloth on an individual as a form of impartation to that person with what God has given me. Your clothing carries your essence. That is why the Bible says that aprons and handkerchiefs were taken from the body of Paul and were taken to the sick, and many of the sick were healed, and demons departed from the afflicted (Acts 19:11-12). Why? The anointing from him passed over the items. When Elisha cried to Elijah, "My father, my father, the chariot of Israel, and the horsemen thereof" (2 Kings 2:12) what happened? The mantle of Elijah fell down. Elisha immediately ripped his own clothes and wore Elijah's mantle. From then on, the anointing of Elijah came upon him in a double measure.

If you are walking in the glory of God and given to prayer and fasting, your clothing will begin to carry the presence and the power of God. On the contrary, someone who is godless has the aura of evil around him. Can you imagine your own daughter or your son exchanging trousers (pants) with a fornicator who is sleeping around? Demons from such person will be transferred to the child. Not too long, that child will be struggling with the demons and may begin to fornicate.

7. Sexual immorality

Sex is the easiest and most common demonic doorway because sex constitutes a blood covenant. Sex is not just an act, it is an impartation. When two people get together in sexual intimacy, they breathe into each other and that becomes a soul exchange. Spirit is breath. It is the quickest, easiest way for spirits to be transferred. That is why the most dangerous bomb on the earth is not an atomic bomb, it is a prostitute. Her ability to move things around for the enemy is powerful. That is why the devil uses the doorway of sex like no other.

I can guarantee that between the ages of five and seven, he will work hard to open that door in the life of a child, either through some relative – an aunty, an uncle, or through some other individual. With such violation, he tries one way or another to open the door and slots his demons there. That demon will produce rebellion, rejection, and sexual promiscuity later as the child enters into teenage years.

Of course, any sex that is not covered by God is a demonic opening. What do I mean by not covered by God? Sex outside of marriage is not covered by God. The only place for sex before God is within the context of marriage. Remember that the Bible says that when Adam and his wife were naked and were not ashamed. Why? God covered them with his glory. When they sinned, that covering was broken and that was why they were looking for fig leaves and accusing one another. Outside of marriage, which is God's purpose, sex is a huge doorway for demons. It is a blood covenant. The exchange of fluid is blood covenant. The breathing on one another is soul impartation. The exchange of fluids and the exchange of breath mean that demons flow back and forth. But, in itself, sex as a covenant means you are swearing (covenanting):

Whatever I am, whatever I will become, whatever I will ever have I give to you, and that person says the same thing to you. The covenant is then sealed by the exchange of body fluids and blood which seals the covenant.

When, for instance, a born again child of God lies with someone to whom they are not married, it is a curse; plus, imagine if that person were to be demonic. The devastation that comes through it is just endless pain. One time in the year 2000, I was preaching at a crusade in Lagos. Every night, after the crusade, the organizers would drive me back to where I was staying. On the way I would see this beautiful, gorgeous, fair-complexioned lady sitting by the wayside. I knew that she was hunting for men; so, on one occasion, I asked the driver to stop the car. She moved to the car and I noticed one of her legs was slightly disabled. I said, "How are you sweetie?" She smiled at me. I started preaching the gospel to her and she got angry. I said, "Well you heard me already. You need to repent and turn your life over to the Lord. Repent or perish." Then, I left.

When I got to where I was staying, as I began to change out of my clothes, there she was! In the spirit I saw her. I said, "The Blood of Jesus!" Then I asked the Lord, "What is happening?" He said, "You thought she was an ordinary girl. She is a Satanist hunting for the destiny of men". That means that any man who slept with her had his destiny vandalized.

Can you imagine people just running around the street picking stuff and not knowing who they are picking? This is why you have to be careful if you have an adulterous partner. Because you are one body, if your partner is committing adultery you will feel it because it is your body out there performing. You have to know the ground you are standing on. That is why one of the sins that God gives as a ground on which He permits divorce is sexual immorality. It is right there in the Word and available if you cannot forgive and get past it. But if you have forgiven it and you are still with the partner, you have to know the Scripture to stand on before you get intimate with your partner again.

The Bible says, "For the unbelieving husband is sanctified by the wife, and the unbelieving wife is sanctified by the husband" (1 Corinthians 7:14). Take an authoritative stand and invoke that Scripture to bind the demons and declare that "my bed is holy, he (or she) is wayward, but I am standing holy for God, so you demons do not touch me!" This helps so that when you get intimate with them, they're not transferring demons to you. Sex is the devil's biggest doorway.

8. Misguided deliverance

Deliverance is by the power of the Holy Spirit. So, when you are spiritually naked, you cannot conduct deliverance. You can become careless and spiritually naked – not just by open sin, but through careless living. If you are not maintaining intimate relationship with the Lord but merely living like an ordinary person, you can become exposed. If you constantly neglect prayer and you do not fast, you can be spiritually naked but still carry the title of a minister of God. When somebody who is an agent of the enemy comes for deliverance after seeing your spiritual state, if you go ahead to minister the deliverance, you may get attacked by demons of lust, for example. And if you do not know your stand you will get in trouble.

There have been deliverance ministers who had gone to minister and ended up sleeping with the person they were supposed to be helping. Those were not accidents. They were attacked and because they were open and naked, it happened to them. I remember, in 1987, there was this young lady in the church. Her parents would send her to me on Saturdays to assist her with her studies. I was still a bachelor, young and nice looking. I was teaching her one day, and she started to attack my genitals with a snake. You do not know these things if you do not have discernment of spirit and you do not live in the Spirit, but I knew.

A man of God without discernment would have begun to react. But I knew what she was doing. I felt the snake hitting my genitals. So I said to her, "Do you want to sleep with your pastor? She said, "Yes". I said, "When I am preaching, do you see the power of God?" She said, "Sure, I do." I said, "Ok, do you think that for thirty minutes of sexual gratification with you I would like to sell the power of God in my life?" She kept quiet. I said, "You need to repent. Take your Bible, go home. See you next week." That ended our Saturday studies.

There are agents of the devil who are out there. Not long ago, God kept saying to me and my wife consistently that there was someone who was going to come and say she needed deliverance, but she would not be truly seeking deliverance; she was an agent of darkness. I would share with my wife and we would talk about it over and again. When the person eventually came, I did not know immediately that it was her. We did deliverance for her, and I embraced her, but did not know.

During my wedding anniversary, our daughter decided to pay for a night for my wife and me to stay at a hotel. We went to the hotel and slept all night. The following day, after being well rested, God opened my eyes. It was as if I was watching TV. I said, "Oh my God, this particular sister is an agent. I saw her right there attacking people in the church". I was already trying to do so much to help her grow in God, but she had no intention of growing. This was not someone you would look at physically and think anything is wrong. From then, I started watching her a little bit more closely. I wouldn't send her away until she figured out that I knew who she was and moved herself away. Until she did, I struggled with the thought of whether to call her and warn her, or just let her go.

I say to people, the devil is joining us in church. Church is not a refuge, it is a battlefront. We are here for one purpose – to get souls saved and delivered. That is why we come, not to eat and drink coffee.

9. Soul ties

What are soul ties? There are positive soul ties and there are negative soul ties. A soul tie is when two souls are intermingled, usually through the gate of love. God instituted soul ties for His purposes. The devil also implements soul ties for his destructive purposes. God will give you covenant friends. That is His investment to making sure His purpose comes to pass in your life. They will love you and give you a commitment that is beyond normal.

If you are not a spiritually mature person, God can put the love of someone in your heart and you will be wondering am I lusting after this person? (if it is someone of opposite gender). If it is a godly soul tie, there is no need to be scared. It is a measure of His purpose within you and the individual. God put that love there. When you pray for them in your prayer time, you will find peace and definition, but on a few occasions you might begin to wonder, am I losing it? Am I going out of boundary? It is not that it is not from God. God can give you that extra bit of love for somebody because there is a measure of His plan and purpose that He is positioning you to carry out in this person's life. This is a positive soul tie.

"Divine love... will never dishonor God."

A classic Biblical example is Jonathan and David. As David came before Saul, Jonathan saw him and loved him. He removed his belt, his girdle, his sword and handed it over to him. That is divine opening, a supernatural love. Over the course of time, they became very close. His father wanted David dead so that Jonathan could be king. He protected David and said, "When you become king, remember me."

Now the devil has his own perverted form of soul ties. It is in the reverse. Where two people are in a lustful relationship, where they cannot part from each other, the two souls have mingled and, because of that, even though things are wrong, they will still stay in that relationship. Through such negative soul ties, demonic flow is easily activated. How do you know that a negative soul tie has occurred between two people? Divine love is a platform for honoring God and fulfilling purpose. It will never dishonor God. When a negative soul tie is enacted between two people they will dishonor God and they will not mind. But real love will never dishonor God, for love is of God.

10. Demonic laying on of hands

One of the things that the enemy does is to quickly push his agents into churches. Can you imagine if God did not give me discernment? I could have fallen victim in so many cases. We started ministry in a particular city, and I met a lady whom I received readily. I remember when she was given the microphone to pray, I thought, "This is a powerful woman; we can just groom her to lead the women's ministry."

She looked like a minister to me. Until we started having a revival and I had the opportunity to take a good look at her. She was wearing snakes. I was shocked. I looked at her and I thought, maybe she only needed deliverance; maybe she was not an agent. But I noticed something else. When I gave her a hug, her hair touched my forehead and I felt some sensations and vibes. Snakes! They tried to stir sensuality in me. I tell you, things happen in the Kingdom. Thank God for Jesus!

Again in her case, two months before she came, the Lord had told my wife that she would be coming and gave a complete description. But this is the funny part; when she came, we did not know right away. But I think it is proper in that way because you do not want to start scanning everyone who comes your way. That is not discernment. That is living in bondage and suspicion. You have to allow everyone to be free and God will inform you at the right moment – this is what I was talking about.

Now, imagine that such an agent sneaked into church. Pastors are constantly looking for helpers and workers. And the thing is, these agents are often very zealous and seemingly ready to render service. You may be thanking God for finally answering your prayers by sending you a responsible worker – not knowing it's a snake you got! Before you know it you are saying, "Let us ordain him a deacon; let us ordain her a deaconess." That is Satan's way of promoting such people over others. From then on, they will start attacking the prayer life of the church; they will start attacking the members so that they become sluggish spiritually. They wouldn't know what hit them.

Supposing you are having a revival and you invite such agents to be laying hands with you. What do you think they will be doing? Transferring demons to people!

FALLEN GENERALS

Demonic laying on of hands can also be from people I call fallen generals. I met a popular man of God in Atlanta and, immediately, the Holy Spirit showed me one or two things. He wanted to come and minister in my church. He asked when I held Bible studies and I told him on Fridays. He said "OK, I will be there."

The man came and spoke powerfully. The following day, I allowed him and he spoke powerfully. I even gave him some good money from the church. We, however, noticed that while the message was going on, he was openly flirting with somebody in the service. I play a lot, but there is a difference between playing and flirtation. The following day, Monday, I was driving around with my daughter and one other person in my car. I said to them, "Mommy and I do not have time to eat now; we will just drop you off at the restaurant and you eat."

My daughter and that other person told us later that when they entered the restaurant, they were shocked that the lady the so-called minister was openly flirting with during ministration and the man of God were in the restaurant having dinner. I was shocked. Somebody he just met in my church the previous day for the first time? I called the sister and said, "How is it that this man, while he was preaching, was flirting with you and on Monday you are having dinner with him?" She said, "Well, he took my number and called me to say he wants to marry me. I am sorry I went out of the way, but I really wanted to know who this guy is. He was sitting there proposing marriage to me, but I told him you just saw me three days ago for the first time in your life."

I decided to take a closer look; so I began to investigate him on the Internet. I found enough. I called the pastor who introduced us and I said, "When I meet people through you, I want to know that they are exactly like you. This man is not like you." She apologized and said she met him through a great international man of God. But he was not who he claimed to be. He had great knowledge of the Word of God. He could recite the entire Bible by heart. Listening to him, you would know that this was no ordinary man, but someone who should be really far up there. A mighty general for God. But he was nowhere. Now, it is one thing for someone to make a mistake and be heartbroken and say, "God, I am sorry." But it is quite another thing to be living a double life deliberately, knowingly. That is the kind of person that demons will flow through. As he lays hands, he starts imparting the mess that is in him to others.

11. Inherited family curses

There are certain families in which you can see a curse operating. How do you know when there is a curse operating? It is usually the same kind of sickness striking different members of the family. This one dies of cancer, the other one is dying of cancer, and another one has died of cancer. There is an existing curse. Or it could be that the family members reach a particular place of prosperity and everything begins to go down. You can see the repeated experiences in each of them. That is an indication of a hidden curse. Or across the board, marriages do not work. This could simply be an existing curse that needs to be broken for the members of the family to be free.

What are the root causes of inherited family curses that can bring this dimension of oppression? Idol worship or idolatry; demonic worship or involvement in demonic rituals and satanic programs; curses pronounced on the family by a person with a demonic authority; as well as cultures and cultural practices that flow from demonic origins and sources, among others.

Chapter Nine

CAN A CHRISTIAN BE DEMON-POSSESSED?

This is a very sensitive issue and one that has been mostly controversial. It actually tends to put people off the benefits of deliverance ministry.

Now, when people say a Christian cannot be demon-possessed, they are correct, in a certain scriptural sense. Getting a demon out of a Christian does not mean that such a believer in Jesus Christ is or was demon-possessed. Very often, when the power of God's Holy Spirit is present and moving to dislodge demons in the oppressed, unenlightened Church members recoil, thinking those receiving help are not true Christians. Nothing could be further from the truth.

Ignorance about deliverance and cleansing is what predisposes well-meaning individuals to despise those who are seeking help and reject deliverance ministration, thinking those receiving help must not be true people of God to have been hosting demons. A born again child of God cannot be demon possessed; however, a born again, spirit-filled, God-fearing, God-honoring child of God can host or have a demon or several, hundreds, even thousands of demons in their lives oppressing them.

God wants His people delivered and free indeed. Where the power of God typically initiates the process of deliverance and, depending on the severity of each case, you will have manifestations. Manifestations include visible shaking, foaming at the mouth, yawning, or rolling on the ground. All these indicate something positive. First, it indicates that the Spirit of God wants to bring about deliverance because, according to His wisdom, deliverance is possible. But the issues have to be worked out for effective deliverance to take place.

Now to stay on track, what does it mean to be demon-possessed? To be demon-possessed means that a particular demon is within the spirit of an individual and therefore has claim of ownership over that person. It is a term that is very difficult to properly apply to any human being, much less a Christian. However, for somebody who has not received Jesus Christ, his spirit automatically belongs to the devil. Man is made of spirit, soul, and body, in that order - the spirit being the most important, because it is the dwelling home of God.

The soul of man is his personality, comprising the mind for reasoning, the will for decisions and the emotions for affection. The mind further consists of imaginations and thought processes for seeing within the eye-gate of the mind in the course of reasoning, making decisions and processing of information.

Man also has a body. A body simply houses the man as long as he lives on the earth. The body has five senses – taste, sight, smell, hearing and touch, which enable him to communicate with his immediate environment. When somebody has not yet received Jesus Christ, the total man – spirit, soul, and body - is under darkness, due to the fall of Adam and due to the fact that man is conceived in iniquity. This is when the devil can effectively possess and control the person

David said, "Behold, I was shapen in iniquity; and in sin did my mother conceive me" (Psalm 51:5). Every person who comes into this world is spiritually dead on arrival and this has been so from the time of the fall of Adam. But when they come to Christ, they are passed from death to life. The Lord Jesus said in John 5:24: "Verily, verily, I say unto you, He that heareth my word, and believeth on him that sent me, hath everlasting life, and shall not come into condemnation; but is passed from death unto life."

When somebody is dead in sin and trespasses, not having come to the Lord, the motions of sin, the power of the grave, and the forces of darkness that are distributed throughout the earth, maintain a major ancestral and territorial control over the individual. As I said before, an individual can be opened to direct demonic activity through the work of the parents or through the things the parents believed and participated in. I have found that even children who are still in the womb can be exposed to demonic infestation. From when they are born and as they grow up, depending on their environment, they can become further exposed to demonic infestation.

A DEMON CANNOT POSSESS A TRUE CHRISTIAN

However, when somebody acknowledges and receives Jesus Christ, demons cannot live in his spirit because eternal life has come into the spirit of that man. That eternal life is superior to the highest power of the enemy which is death. Resurrection life comes into that spirit, and darkness is dispelled and the light of God is maintained by the Holy Spirit in the heart of the individual. That is why the Bible says that if a man has not the spirit of Christ he is not of Jesus Christ (Romans 8:9). In other words, if you have received Christ Jesus, if you know Him as your Lord and Savior, the Spirit of Christ comes to indwell your spirit. But He does not just indwell - He first regenerates; that is, gives life, the God-kind of life, to your human spirit, and then dwells in your human spirit. At that point in time, neither Lucifer, nor death, nor hell, nor any other power can reside in the spirit of that man. That man belongs to Christ completely – spirit, soul, and body and cannot be said to be demon-possessed.

However, depending on what the individual had been exposed to previously, and depending on whether they had received appropriate help as they integrated into Christianity, that person can still host thousands of demon spirits in their body and aspects of the soul already violated and scarred. In other words, the demons do not possess that believer, but aspects of that believer's life have been demonized. This is what has to be addressed through deliverance ministry; through counseling and training in the Word of God, to reclaim aspects of human personality and behavior, which have

"A demon cannot possibly own a Christian because a Christian already belongs to the Lord Jesus."

been corrupted by evil powers that were there prior to coming to the Lord. That is what we address in deliverance, and to that extent, we cannot say that a believer is demon-possessed; rather it is a form of oppression being outside of the spirit of man.

I once ran a church in a certain neighborhood on the penthouse floor of an eight-story building. It was a lovely chapel. We enjoyed it, until one day, we found, to our amazement, that we were invaded by fast-moving, smart little mice. It was big trouble most especially for the sisters. You can just imagine a sister coming to the office and this little mouse shows up, bumps us, and runs around. Some would scream, some would jump on the chairs. It was quite interesting to say the least. Would you therefore say, at this point in time, that my church was owned by the mice? This is what it implies when someone says possession suggests ownership.

A demon cannot possibly own a Christian because a Christian already belongs to the Lord Jesus. The mice were in the church, moving around, and we had to deal with them. The mice did not possess the church. The church, at that particular time, possessed some mice because the church was housing some mice. That is the proper word. A Christian can be "housing" demon spirits, of which they may not be aware immediately. Because those demons are able to stay undercover, they can gradually destroy the benefits and the peace of that individual believer. However, the purpose of deliverance is to locate the demons, either by the anointing or by the gift of the Spirit, called discerning of spirits, or even by mature counseling and observation. When we see certain types of behaviors which do not subscribe to the Word of God on a pronounced basis – I call them exaggerated behavior due to demonic corruption - we can then bring those people into counseling and get the demons to leave.

ONLY BELIEVERS CAN RECEIVE DELIVERANCE

Another way to answer this question is to inquire: Can you cast a demon out of somebody who is not a believer? The answer will be no. You cannot really cast out a demon from somebody who is not a believer because Jesus already indicated that when an unclean spirit is gone out of a person, he walks about in dry places seeking rest and finds none (Matthew 12). This means that demons are spirits without bodies that try to find homes in any individual they are able to invade and then manifest their evil nature. When you get rid of them, they become tormented and wander around like homeless people. Then these demons decide to return to their original abode with stronger assistants. They record easy success if the place is found empty, and the last stage of the person becomes worse than the first.

This indicates that, for an individual who is not willing to be submitted to the lordship of Jesus Christ and become His disciple, it is useless to try to get demons out of them because we will actually complicate their already bad conditions. This is why I say often that you cannot deliver anybody who is not already delivered. In other words, what we call deliverance - which I will more appropriately call cleansing - is cleaning out demons from an individual. That cleansing is actually only applicable to people who have made a profession of faith and are ready to be disciples of the Lord. These are the people you can cast demons out of. Your casting demons out of them simply means you are enforcing the law over these demons because as soon as people receive the Lord Jesus Christ, they are His property and any demon that remains in that individual is in violation or committing spiritual territorial trespassing. Any child of God who is conscious of the authority of Christ that has been delegated to them can cast out that devil and get rid of it.

A Christian cannot be demon-possessed and deliverance cannot be done on the unbeliever. That being the case, we can conclude that deliverance is the bread of children. There is a case of the Syrophoenecian woman in Matthew 15, who was not in the Abrahamic covenant, but who, during the ministry of Jesus went after Him, desiring deliverance for her daughter who was demon tormented. The Bible says the Lord would not answer her and she followed hard after Him. When her persistence became unbearable, the disciples complained to the Lord. He replied, "I am not sent but unto the lost sheep of the house of Israel."

In other words, in His first coming, His ministry was primarily to the house of Israel. But the woman pressed on in faith. So, Jesus turned to her and said, "It is not meet to take the children's bread, and to cast it to dogs." Remarkably, the woman answered in faith; she didn't feel insulted having just been called a dog by the Lord Jesus. She said, "Truth, Lord: yet the dogs eat of the crumbs which fall from their masters' table." She was simply saying, "I am not asking for real bread, just give me the crumbs. Whether bread or crumbs it still has enough power to cast out the devil."

Here, we see that deliverance is called the children's bread. Of course, Jesus was impressed by the woman's faith and said, "O woman, great is thy faith: be it unto thee even as thou wilt." From that hour, the demon left. The most important point here is that deliverance is called the bread of children. So we can conclude that deliverance is for God's children. The unsaved person cannot rightly benefit from deliverance.

As I have explained before, the Bible says that we have been translated into the Kingdom of God's dear Son, having obtained redemption through His Blood, the forgiveness of sins (Colossians

1:14). There are four classes of spiritual realities from which created beings can function. The lowest level is the man who is in sin and does not know the Lord Jesus Christ. Such a person runs around with a dead spirit. Immediately above that is the kingdom of darkness where we have Lucifer, the leader of that gang of rebels, the other fallen angels (in the categories of principalities, powers, rulers of darkness, and hosts of spiritual wickedness in high places). Then there are men, who are vested with satanic authority, also functioning at the level of the rebellious one being alienated from the life of God. The third category of spirits are the angels that have not rebelled but are still with God who are in superior position now and have authority over the kingdom of darkness. They serve God, God's Family, and God's Kingdom. Finally, we have the highest class of spirit beings, Father, Son, and Holy Spirit. Every person who is born again is a part of this Family of God. That is the superior class.

BELIEVERS CARRY GOD'S DNA

I say superior because every born-again person carries God's DNA; they carry the divine nature and have escaped corruption by becoming partakers of the divine nature. It puts us even in a superior class to the angels. This is not to be disrespectful to the phenomenal work that the angels of God do, but that is the truth. The angels are God's servants (Hebrews 1:7). They are sent forth to minister for the heirs of salvation (Hebrews 1:14). If you are born again, you are an heir of salvation, a joint heir with Christ; you are in a family relationship with The Almighty God - God is your Father and His DNA resides in you.

What I wish to emphasize with the above explanation is that demon-possession is far from Christians. However, Christians who are born again and made partakers of the divine nature, filled with the Holy Spirit and walking in the will of God, can also, in fact, have thousands of demons in various aspects of their lives, depending on what they had been exposed. At the point they become Christians, those things ought to be cleaned out so that they can serve the Lord meaningfully.

BELIEVERS CAN HAVE DEMONS

We see a very parallel example in the Bible in the deliverance of the demon oppressed man of Gadara in Luke 8:26-39. Gadara is a part of Israel. When Israel came out of Egypt, two and a half tribes inherited the Amorite kings and possessed the first set of inheritance before everybody crossed over Jordan to possess the Land of Canaan. These two and a half tribes always seemed to be having trouble aligning spiritually and theologically with the other nine and a half tribes. At a point in time, their spiritual condition deteriorated. Until even the time of the ministry of Jesus, they were openly raising swine and thriving in the swine business which was forbidden to the Jewish people.

Here, in Luke 8, we find a man who was possessed by a legion of demons. A legion is at least 6,800 demons. This possessed man was a son of Abraham, within the Abrahamic covenant; yet he was possessed to such a level with that many demons in him. What did Jesus do? In fact, the man initiated the actions, because this man who was carrying close to 7000 demons or more, had enough sense to run to Jesus and worship Him. His tormented soul could still recognize his Maker and he worshiped the Lord Jesus - whereas many religious, self-righteous people were in the temple, persecuting the Lord throughout His ministry. It was in such scenario that Jesus challenged the demons to get out of the man, and with His command and glorious presence, He cleaned out the entire haul of demons from this man.

Can you imagine what would have happened if Jesus had not addressed those demons but just accepted the worship and the man became His follower? It would have happened that some days the man would demonstrate sanity, but on other days, he would act insanely.

There are many in Christianity who have dual characters: bipolar characters. One day, they are good Christians; at another time, you find them behaving strangely. One day, they are very good parents; another day, they are just pure evil. This is a sign that something is tormenting and working there to tear down their Christian profession and to torment them and those who are close to them. Often, when we discover people like that in the church, we just counsel them. We do not pray or fast to discern what is actually producing this type of behavior and to get to the root of it.

I remember some years ago there was this wonderful individual who was so kind to us. However, at some point, I realized that this wonderful child of God who was so good to us, walking in holiness and devoted to God, had some demonic undercurrents which were undermining her effectiveness and actually had substantially destroyed some of her blessings. I requested her to join me on a seven-day fast, where we could pray for eliminating what I thought I saw. We embarked on the fast and at the end, when I wanted to pray, the demon surfaced and tried to feed my pride by shouting that I was too tough for it; that it had cleverly concealed its behavior hiding itself all this time, and now I had come to expose it. I answered that I was not the tough one; it was the Lord Jesus who had the stronger power.

Demons can be very clever and subtle. They can be in a Christian and carefully dodge the fire. What will happen is that these

Christians will be very zealous and will work very hard for God; but every time that the demon knows that they will be face-to-face with fire, it manipulates their circumstances so that they are not in those meetings. This can go on for years. What the demon is doing is simply protecting itself from the line of fire. But if by some divine intervention the individual is exposed to the firepower of the Holy Spirit in an atmosphere that is charged, what happens is that the demon is forced to appear and flee.

It is a very embarrassing situation for the devil because his well-conceived agenda of destruction is brought to the open and his weakness is exposed as his demons bow out under the superior firepower of the Holy Spirit and the Almighty name of the Lord Jesus Christ.

I will say conclusively that, according to the Word of God, a born again Christian cannot be demon-possessed. That is the final word. But a Christian can be oppressed, he can be suppressed, he can be obsessed, he can be depressed. These are demonic conditions. They are abnormal and they are to be addressed by the Word of God.

Chapter Ten

SEVEN IMPORTANT MESSAGES TO THE CHURCH

S ome time ago, the Lord called my attention and gave me these seven points to deliver to His Body, the Church. According to what the Lord said, if these seven things are not handled carefully, then the charismatic Pentecostal church will become like semi-occult churches. So, we are to pay attention to these, so that the devil, our enemy, will not be able to destroy the Church from within.

JESUS CHRIST IS THE MESSAGE OF THE ENTIRE BIBLE

From Genesis to Revelation, God the Father, through God the Holy Spirit, is presenting revelations of His Son. The Lord Jesus Christ is who God wants to reveal. He wants us to see His Son who He loves so much and is willing to deliver up for our sins. Whatever topics we preach - whether salvation, prosperity, deliverance, healing or breakthrough - we must reckon with the fact that the revelation of Jesus Christ is the message of gospel. If Jesus Christ had not come in the flesh to be born, suffer, die and be raised again from the dead, there would have been no message to preach, no ministry, no church, no minister. The Person of the Lord needs to feature prominently in our messages and songs. God wants the whole world to know His magnificent Son. This is the burden of the Almighty! How desperately today's Church need to return to that simplicity of the gospel and present Jesus Christ and Him crucified.

REDEMPTION IS BY THE BLOOD

The foundation of true Christianity is the testimony of Blood of the Son of God. He is the Lamb slain from the foundation of the world. We are not dealing with blood of a mere human being; not blood of animals, but the Blood of the Son of the Living God. The Blood of Jesus is central to the Gospel message, because without the shedding of Blood there is no remission or removal of sin.

It is the Blood of Jesus that enables God Almighty in His glory and holiness to be able to look upon a vile sinner and remove his sin. Without the Blood, the Church will fall into the trap of New Age thinking. The Bible says that without the shedding of blood there is no remission (Hebrews 9:22). More particularly in these days when there is a surge in wickedness, evil, and satanic activities, the Church of God needs to bring forth the testimony of the Blood, as it is by means of this Blood we overcome the evil one (Revelation 12:11).

Without the Blood, the message of repentance will be lost, as it is the Blood that encourages us to come into a place of humbleness, brokenness, and repentance. The shedding of the Blood of Jesus presupposes that man is a fallen creature and helpless to save himself so the Son of God paid our ransom

THE CROSS

The Cross as a message and lifestyle is at the heart of the Gospel. If the Church of the Living God does not pay attention and bring back the message of the Cross, we become a generation who will be mostly emotional but cannot take a stand for righteousness. By means of that ugly Cross, God's Best was crucified. By means of that Cross, we are crucified to the world and the world is crucified to us. The Cross brings us to the place of self-denial. If we do not come to the place of self-denial, we will only have an academic Christianity that cannot be respected by God and which cannot impress the devil. God doesn't mind how much we sing about His love for us (which is real anyway), but He just wants us to be like Him and the Cross forces us to embrace the narrow way in our lives.

> *"For the preaching of the cross is to them that perish foolishness; but unto us which are saved it is the power of God" (1Corinthians 1:18).*

The Church must return to simple messages on the Cross.

INTIMACY WITH GOD

God not only loves us; God is in love with us. The Lord God wants to be with His people. At one point, He told me that He would allow the Holy Spirit to take the love between Himself and Jesus and transmit it to the Church. When He said that, all the glory of heaven was unleashed upon me; I was melting where I was.

God wants us to hunger and thirst for Him. David cried out, "O God, thou art my God; early will I seek thee: my soul thirsteth for thee, my flesh longeth for thee in a dry and thirsty land, where no water is" (Psalm 63:1). We must return to a place of intimacy with our God. It is a privilege for us to love Him, because He first loved us. The message and lifestyle of intimacy with God will open the door to new possibilities in the supernatural realm of Almighty God. We at the church of God must return to the message of intimacy and the pursuit of God. Let us love Him, let us chase after Him. He delights in it.

THE POWER OF THE ALMIGHTY

When we become intimate with God, we enter into the power side of the Almighty. The gospel is not in mere words. It is also in demonstration of the Spirit and of the power. This generation cannot be saved with philosophy and sound doctrines alone. This generation must be confronted with the raw power of God. That is what God is calling us to – to embrace His power. As we get intimate with Him and He begins to adjust us, we will move into the realm of power. The age in which we live has seen an upsurge in counterfeit power in all shapes and forms invading all religions. The devil is anxious to take over, but it is not his time. This is the time that God wants to raise a glorious Church, put His seal of authority on the sons and daughters of the Living God who will be able to give this generation a demonstration of the resurrection power of the Lord Jesus.

This is the desire of the Lord. Go for the power of the Holy Spirit. It will take power to break shackles, to bring changes, to transform societies and nations. God said to tell His children to desire power. He warned me in a revelation that the power of the Holy Spirit would be decisive and that those who do not pay the price to walk in His power would live as beggars, because all His provisions would flow from His power to His children.

EVANGELISM

Power is for purpose. Power without purpose is abuse and ultimate destruction. God wants us to evangelize, to craft ways and means to reach the lost, to spend our time and our money to reach the lost. If the Church of the present day does not rise up to reach out to the lost the consequence will be that we will be hardened in our consciences. We will be practicing self-hypnosis, that is – we will be so concerned about our own needs to the point that we will not see what God has done. In the wilderness, God sent the Israelites manna every day. When that day's supply was done, they forgot about it. He had to send it again the next morning, and by the evening they had forgotten again and rebelled. Miracles without focus on the purpose of evangelism will lead to hardness of heart. God wants His Church to return to the purpose for which he came, which is to seek and save that which was lost.

ETERNITY

Most Christians are living from time to eternity, and that is wrong. God invites us to live in eternity now. Once you are born again, you do not wait to die to enjoy eternity. You are in eternity now. What is the advantage of living from eternity through6 time? That way, you are judging yourself day to day. People are so blessed today that they enjoy the blessing and forget that heaven is their home. What will it benefit us if we gain the whole world and lose our souls? By living in eternity, we will be able to shun sinful behavior and avoid the traps that Satan puts all over the place by way of temptation. We will be able to live an accountable life, always cognizant that we are pilgrims on the earth, hasting unto the day of the Lord, putting all our energy knowing that heaven is real. Sin will not be able to overtake us.

These are the seven urgent messages the Lord wants the Church to reckon with. If you are reading this, God bless you!

APPENDIX

SOME HELPFUL PRAYER POINTS

DELIVERANCE PRAYER POINTS (1)

1. Lord Jesus Christ, I know You are real! Make Yourself known to me in a deep, personal, and new way like never before.

2. Remove the veil of darkness (Religion, Demons and Flesh) that stands in my way. Oh God, let the light of Your glory in the face of Jesus burn away every form of darkness that seeks to hold me back from perfect knowledge and experience of who You truly are.

3. Lord God, I desire and pray to know You and be filled completely with Your love that far surpasses human ability to understand. I ask to be made complete in Your own love.

4. Father of Love, life, and light, strip away from my life, every limiting self-imposed notion of You that is incorrect. Let Your perfect and complete love that heals set me free to be all that You created me to be.

5. Father of life, I surrender myself completely to You today. Let the River of Your Love and Joy overwhelm me and take me past my fears, hesitations, hurts, memories of abuse, pains and channel the currents of my life into meaning fulfilment of my destiny.

6. Lord Jesus Christ, I pray that as I read this book on Deliverance, Faith and Love will be my guiding principle and Your Blessed Holy Spirit will bring me into unique understanding.

7. Finally, in the mighty name of Jesus Christ, I declare according to the Word of God that I am who God says I am and that every devil in hell is subject unto me through the Mighty Name of my Lord and Savior Jesus Christ.

DELIVERANCE PRAYER POINTS (2)

1. Lord God my Savior, I love and adore You. I completely renounce all hidden things of darkness in my life and destiny.

2. Precious Father of light, let Your light expose and rebuke every layer of darkness in my life. `

3. Lord God, in the precious Name of Jesus, confront any hold of darkness in my life and set me free from satanic yokes, burdens, and limitations in the mighty name of the Lord Jesus Christ.

4. I receive the God kind of faith to confront and defeat every satanic investment in my body, life and destiny in the mighty name of Jesus.

5. I apply the blood of Jesus Christ to neutralize every satanic covenant in my life and declare such evil covenants nullified, broken and destroyed in the mighty name of Jesus

DELIVERANCE PRAYER POINTS (3)

1. Thank the Lord for the understanding of what deliverance is.

2. Decree aloud: I have come to Mount Zion; today I embrace my deliverance and declare my deliverance a living reality in the Mighty name of Jesus.

3. I acknowledge, confess and renounce every sin that exposed me to defilement and I repent of them (name all known sins

and receive forgiveness and cleansing in the Mighty name of Jesus Christ).

4. I renounce every evil covenant existing in my life, home, family; I release the fire of God to consume every token in my life, giving the enemy legal right over me in Jesus' name.

5. I declare I am a blood bought child of God and the Blood of the everlasting Covenant speaks on my behalf. (Hebrews 9:12 and Hebrews 13:20)

6. I stand on my Blood Covenant with the Lord Jesus Christ today to renounce any evil covenant upon my life. I denounce any satanic covenant and command the curse to be broken and lifted in the mighty name of Jesus

7. Sovereign Lord, mark me this day with the true spirit of consecration and separation from sin.

8. I take my place as the 'Joseph' of my family and declare I am the curse breaker and the reproach remover in my family in the mighty name of the Lord Jesus Christ.

DELIVERANCE PRAYER POINTS (4)

1. Heavenly Father, I thank You for the sacrifice of the Lord Jesus on my behalf. I declare with my mouth, what I now firmly believe in my heart that Jesus Christ is the sinless holy Son of God who came into this world to pay the price for my sin. I believe in His Virgin birth, atoning death, burial, and resurrection by the glory of the Father on the third day. I further declare Jesus as my personal Savior and the Lord of all my life.

2. Standing in faith before the Throne of God, the Father, Son, and Holy Spirit, the eternal witness of the Blood of Sprinkling, the elect Angels and all the hosts of heaven, I declare the Lordship of the Lord Jesus Christ over my life and destiny. I declare I am born of God and have His DNA.

3. I declare aloud before the entire kingdom of darkness, Satan, principalities and powers of darkness that I now belong to Jesus Christ and therefore renounce all allegiance to evil covenants and commitments. From this moment any satanic claims against me is made void by the Blood of Jesus and therefore illegal and subject to divine judgement and retribution.

4. I receive the spirit of wisdom and understanding regarding my role in life and destiny and full understanding of the deliverance process and where I stand in God's victory in the mighty name of Jesus Christ.

5. Heavenly Father, strengthen me; train my hands to war, impart a victory mentality to me continually, and help me to abide in your love.

6. Lord God, help me to know Your purpose for my life and fill my soul with passion to fulfill it in the mighty name of Jesus

7. Precious Father of light, help me to function at a spiritual level of understanding that effectively neutralizes satanic temptations, persecutions, and blackmail in the mighty name of Jesus Christ

DELIVERANCE PRAYER POINTS (5)

1. Almighty Father of all spirits. You are the Lord God who alone delivers. I submit all aspects of my life to the glorious operations of your eternal Spirit. Release my soul and my life from every satanic yokes, weights and liabilities in the mighty name of Jesus.

2. Covenant Making and Keeping God; I invoke the power of your blood Covenant in my life to nullify any illegal claims the devil and his co-horts are seeking to enforce in my life and family.

3. My God and King, I fully recognize the operation of your hands in my life; so, build me up. Visit every aspect of my life

with new mercies today in the mighty name of Jesus Christ.

4. Lord God, grant me a bigger picture of how big you are and help me to define and understand my purpose and role in my destiny and your kingdom.

5. I declare boldly that the light of the glorious gospel of the Lord Jesus Christ is shining brightly in my heart and every satanic lies and strongholds on my mind is exposed and destroyed permanently in the mighty name of Jesus Christ.

DELIVERANCEPRAYER POINTS (6)

1. Every demonic corruption in my character be exposed now and destroyed in the name of Jesus. I decree that as I have borne the image of the first Adam; so shall I now bear in my mortal body the branding of the Lord Jesus Christ.

2. Heavenly Father, cleanse, heal and set me free from any compulsive and addictive behavior in the mighty name of the Lord Jesus Christ.

3. In the mighty name of Jesus Christ, I decree that any channel, connection to and flow of evil into my life be disrupted now, cut off and permanently destroyed.

4. Sovereign Lord, I submit myself for a deep work of the cross in my life. Let every corruption in my flesh and exaggerated aspects of my character due to demonic undercurrents be corrected, reclaimed and harmonized with your divine nature in the mighty name of Jesus.

DELIVERANCE PRAYER POINTS (7)

1. Today in the mighty name of Jesus, I ---- take my proper place in life and Destiny; I take my place before God, in my family as a priest and curse breaker, in society as a community builder and in the Church of God as a Kingdom builder. I take my

appoint places in destiny and declare I am God's shining light in my generation!

2. I here and now repent for and renounce every demonic opened door in my life and family. Today, I fire every satanic power operating these doors and slam them shut permanently in the mighty name of Jesus Christ. Heavenly Father, I invite you to come through these doors yourself and because you have come through them today, they are hallowed and no satanic power is permitted to operate them again forever in the mighty name of Jesus

3. I declare my total freedom from the unfruitful works of darkness today. The son of perdition has no common grounds with me. I declare my life a no safe zone for demonic activity. I am the light of Jesus Christ in my generation and as such, I fully embrace my responsibility to so shine, repel darkness and glorify my Father in Heaven. Thank you JESUS, I love you!!!

4. Declare aloud: Heavenly Father, I give You praise for the new covenant with You. I renounce the devil and all his demons in every area of my life. From today I will live my life for Jesus. I receive the life of Christ; I shall not die but live. With my whole life, I will serve You forever and be an instrument of deliverance to others in Jesus' name. Amen

5. Lord God, I repent and renounce every connection and exposures that channel the flow of evil into my life. From today, cleanse, sanctify and season every part of my life by fire in the mighty name of Jesus Christ.

DELIVERANCE PRAYER POINTS (8)

1. I decree and declare that I am a blood bought child of the living God and the Blood of the Everlasting Covenant is active in my life. Every operation of the Kingdom of darkness against me is illegal and therefore it shall not stand nor come

to pass in the mighty name of Jesus.

2. I command all evil altars of sin, affliction, captivity, and bondage in my life to burn to ashes right now in Jesus' name.

3. I plead the Blood of Jesus upon me and upon every part of my body and every area of my life. Let the Blood of Jesus, cleanse me now from every contamination with evil in Jesus' name. Holy Spirit of the living God, I invite you afresh to take your rightful place my life. Holy Spirit, deliver me. Purify my soul and sanctify me in Jesus' name.

4. I declare that I am holy for I am the righteousness of God in Christ.

5. I command my stolen opportunities and possessions to locate me from today. Whatever I lost in my time of bondage and captivity, I recover all now in the mighty name of Jesus Christ. Give God thanks and quality praise.

DELIVERANCE PRAYER POINTS (9)

"Shake thyself from the dust; arise, and sit down, O Jerusalem: loose thyself from the bands of thy neck, O captive daughter of Zion" (Isaiah 52:2).

1. I shake myself from every dust of my past failures and defeat; I break the grip of every satanic limitation and restriction in the mighty name of Jesus' Amen

2. I release the fire of the Holy Spirit to destroy every fire that is keeping me down and bound; I set ablaze every anti-progress spells of the enemy in my life and command divine supernatural acceleration in all my life endeavors in the mighty name of Jesus'

3. I command every power scattering/wasting my resources/opportunities to expire in Jesus' name. Amen

4. I hereby decree that I shall no longer serve sin and my

oppressors in Jesus' name. Amen.

5. Every power suppressing my divine elevation, be destroyed now; I embrace my moment in the limelight in Jesus' name.

DELIVERANCE PRAYER POINTS (10)

1. Every power in me resisting and hating deliverance, be exposed and destroyed now by the Blood of Jesus.

2. Every grave clothes and evil objects the enemy is using as points of contact to oppress, suppress, depress and obsess me, catch fire now in Jesus' name. Amen

3. Every contamination in my life be cleansed with the Blood of Jesus.

4. My stolen, destroyed, or killed glory, I command you now to come alive in Jesus' name. Amen

5. My Father, preserve my spirit, soul and body blameless, unto the coming of our Lord Jesus Christ. Amen.

BIBLOGRAPHY

Watchman Nee, (January 1980) The Latent Power of the Soul. Christian Fellowship Publishers Inc., New York

Derek Prince; (1998) They Shall Expel Demons (Your Invisible Enemies) Bakers Publishing Group, Ada Michigan.

John Simpson and Edmund Weiner (Editors) Oxford English Dictionary Online. Oxford University Press Publication. 1989

Eto Victoria, Lesson Notes on Deliverance; (1986) Shalom Christian Mission, Ozoro, Delta State, Nigeria.

Hinn Benny, (2011) Angels and Demons, Bookmark Publishing Dallas, Texas USA

Obode O. Jerome, 90 Keys to Effective Praying AuthorHouse, UK

ABOUT THE AUTHOR

Patrick I. Odigie is a man graced with extraordinary prophetic insights, revelations, and his ministry is marked by signs, wonders, and demonstrations of the Spirit. The Ministry of this Apostolic Prophet, spanning three decades, has taken him to four Continents and he is mandated by God to mobilize the Praying Power of the Church to unleash end-time revival and Healing of the Nations. Patrick Odigie functions under a powerful anointing of Counsel, revelations, dreams interpretations and encounters in the spirit realm.

He is a trained Deliverance minister, substance abuse counselor and a consultant/participant at World Forum of Drug Demand Reduction, Bangkok, Thailand, in December 1994 under the auspices of United Nations Drug Control Program for Non-Governmental Organizations. Brother Odigie is an alumnus of the prestigious Haggai Institute of Advanced Christian Leadership, Maui, Hawaii.

He presently resides in Uniondale New York where He Oversees the Prophetic Power house Ministries; and travels extensively throughout the Nation mobilizing churches and Christian fellowship groups to unleash the power of the praying church for end-time healing revival. The three cord focus of his message is Prayer, Sacrifice, and Intimacy with the Holy Spirit as pre-requisites for accessing the power of God for the end-time healing revival.

He sees himself as an extreme lover of Jesus, and seeks to promote a spirit of bridal love for the Lord everywhere. Patrick is married to his best friend, Pastor Mabel Odigie, and is blessed with three anointed and prophetic children; Praise, Honor and Favor.

www.ingramcontent.com/pod-product-compliance
Lightning Source LLC
Chambersburg PA
CBHW071118090426
42736CB00012B/1937